the **soft furnishings**
source book

the **soft furnishings**
source book

Leslie Geddes-Brown

with step-by-step projects by **Lucinda Ganderton**

RYLAND
PETERS
& SMALL

London   New York

Senior designer Sally Powell

Senior editor Henrietta Heald

Location research manager Kate Brunt

Location researcher Sarah Hepworth

Picture researcher Jenny Drane

Production Patricia Harrington

Art director Gabriella Le Grazie

Publishing director Alison Starling

Illustration Lizzie Sanders

Specially commissioned photography

David Montgomery; styling Serena Hanbury

Index Alison Bravington

First published in the United Kingdom in 2001
by Ryland Peters & Small
Kirkman House
12–14 Whitfield Street
London W1T 2RP
www.rylandpeters.com

10 9 8 7 6 5 4 3 2 1

ISBN 1 84172 118 2

A CIP record for this book is available from
the British Library.

Printed and bound in China

contents

introduction

Take a plain cube of a room. Paint it a soft neutral grey, with matt-white ceiling, door and skirtings, and more of the same on the surrounds of the Georgian sash windows. The floor is made of softly polished wood. Here is a perfect space in which to experiment with what fabrics can do for a room.

You want to be minimalist? Add a pair of leather Wassily chairs designed by Marcel Breuer in 1925, a fireplace carved halfway up the wall (like Peter Mandelson's), a set of Rupert Spira pots and, on the wall, a Yoruba narrowstrip textile in ochre, terracotta, black and dark vermilion.

Swedish? Put in a curved hardback settle with cabriole legs and cover it with square cushions in pink and grey stripes and checks. Put a round-bellied longcase clock against one wall and, at the windows, hang sheer white linens in front of blinds in a variation on the pink and grey cushions.

For a French room, you could substitute gilded fauteuils and change the clock for a wood and ormolu pillar timepiece on a bracket. Instead of checks and stripes, the chairs could be upholstered in rose-madder toile de Jouy and the windows given generous curtains of the same pictorial cotton backed by a checked toile de Nîmes.

An English Regency room would return to generous stripes – but, unlike the Swedish cottons, these would be a twilled silk in vibrant colours – black and ultramarine, citrus yellow with scarlet, purple and emerald green. The furniture, upholstered in shades of these colours, or embroidered with gros and petit point, would be sabre-legged and brass-inlaid, perhaps including a chaise longue with plain silk bolster. The walls would be densely hung with silk-embroidered pictures of flowers and butterflies, and the curtains swagged, tasselled and pelmeted with gilded arrow poles.

That same experimental cube could become a vernacular American parlour, where a traditional log-cabin quilt hangs on the wall behind a painted chest of drawers adorned with a single bird decoy. The curtains are a strong tweedy check in design, but made of cotton woven in browns and greys. Cushions on the hardback chairs are in one of the brown pictorial cottons – closely resembling toile, but showing a glorious scene from the Mexican–American war. There's a rag rug on the floor decorated with the Stars and Stripes.

It's tempting to go on, through Japanese- and Chinese-inspired rooms, to those instigated by India and Africa, by Russia and Italy. But you get the point: a room is only an architectural space if it has no furnishings or fabrics. It only becomes a proper room – your own creation – when soft furnishings are added. They are as important as that.

FABRIC STYLES

From soft neutrals to joyful toiles, from crisp cottons to luscious damasks – what gives a room its character, what can change it utterly, is the choice of fabric and how you use it.

plain colours

Unlike patterns, plain fabrics virtually never go out of fashion – though the colours you choose just may. The secret is to pick complex mixtures of shades and tones or to vary the textures. If your colours are strong or rich, forget about texture; if they are refined and subtle, then look for interesting weaves and slubs.

At the opposite end of the colour spectrum from neutral, plain fabrics ask for the sort of strong colours and colour combinations that have become the hallmark of designers from David Hicks to Tricia Guild. Such professionals would be the first to tell you that achieving results in this area is far from easy. It all depends on colour saturations, levels of blues mixed with reds or reds with yellows. But the theory doesn't really matter. The best way to ensure that these thugs in the colour spectrum behave for you is to mix them together on a colour board and spend days looking at how they work in different lights, in different moods and in different mixtures.

Large areas of strong colour, whether black or chocolate, cerise or tangerine, are the hardest to get right – but with thought and experiment it can be done. Remember that the larger the area of one colour – vermilion curtains on deep Georgian windows, for instance – the more the colour will take over. It may set up reactions with other shades around it, shadowing

OPPOSITE PAGE, LEFT There is only one patterned fabric in this elegant room. The startling zebra stripes contrast with the sleek grey sofa and the minimalist lamp and rug.

OPPOSITE PAGE, RIGHT If you think plain colours are boring, just consider this stunning mixture of soft fruits: raspberry mixed with redcurrant, with a touch of white-currant colouring in the hessian detail on the cushions and in the ropes on the back of the sofa.

LEFT Bold ultramarine holds this charming bedroom together. The checked and striped cushions match the chair's upholstery exactly, and the same shade is picked up in the pretty patchwork quilt that covers the bed.

BELOW This Paris living room relies for its decorative effect on salvaged wood and utterly plain colours. But the combination of off-black, off-white and crimson has a strong abstract quality.

blues into indistinct mauves, making white walls come all over pink. If you want to take this brave course, you may even have to make changes at the last minute. One solution is to proceed one step at a time: find the right red or the right yellow but use it in small amounts – cushions, throws, accessories – until you are sure that you have got it perfect. Buy a length of plain fabric and drape it around the window to get the effect of curtains

FAR LEFT This relaxed room manages to integrate the interior and exterior of the house by using soft greens and floral cotton cushions on the sofa in front of the window. All the colours in the room are in keeping with the features that are visible in the garden.
LEFT It is not a God-given rule that chairs in a dining room should match each other. But this disparate quartet around a table are all upholstered in shades of green which appear elsewhere in the room.

or over the armchairs to see how it would look as loose covers. Be ready to tone down the brightness of your walls and remove all clutter, from small paintings to shelves of books, to achieve the right clarity for your big statement. For big statement this will be. Get it right, and the results will be stunning. Wrong – and the stunning effect will be like a thump on the head and stars circling around the eyes.

Personally, I think it is worth being brave, particularly so if you have a well-proportioned room with good light (views don't matter). Strong colours are also helpful for people who dislike clutter or, for that matter, cannot afford a great deal of furniture. A chair or two covered with scarlet cotton throws, windows framed with bright but unpatterned sari silks, a single green leaf in a vase and one large picture in colours which bring together the entire scheme are all that is needed here.

You can add in any number of neutral shades such as string and cement – they will simply give reassurance. However, if you were to throw a single vermilion cushion into your subtle white-on-white room, it would be like adding a tomato into a basketful of eggs – exciting, but not what you originally intended. The best combinations of colours are often discovered by accident. Try moving cushions, throws and rugs from room to room to see if you can come up with the unexpected.

neutrals and plain weaves

The move towards plain fabrics plainly woven is a reaction to the power-shouldered curtain treatments of the 1980s, when fortunes were spent on buying luxury silks and damasks in such lengths that they trailed uselessly on the floor. The urge to decorate in a succession of neutral shades – bone, string, greige, stone, mouse – followed.

Is it a coincidence that the word 'fash' – meaning 'bother, inconvenience, trouble' – appears directly before 'fashion' in my dictionary? If so, it is perfectly appropriate. In interiors as much as in clothes, fashion is an inconvenience that should, if possible, be avoided. It may not be possible to ignore fashion entirely, but anyone who wants a calm, pleasant and less extravagant life should try to disregard the fads of the moment and look instead at the direction in which the mainstream is leading.

Fashion in soft furnishings is much the same as that in clothes: the taste-makers are looking for innovations, which only they are aware of, while the mass of people trust the big advertisers and the big stores to point them in the right direction – by which time the fashion has usually gone cold.

For several years now, the cognoscenti have been hanging old French linen bedsheets instead of curtains. Stained, patched, amateurishly embroidered in cross-stitch in inconvenient places, these sheets are made of handwoven fabric; the yarn itself is handspun, and even the hems are hand-sewn. This style of material, found only in the most eclectic antique shops for far less money than a designer fabric, is the antithesis of the modern, the smooth, the factory-made – and hence desirable.

The use of either neutral shades or the more vibrant contrast of plain colours demands both subtlety and restraint. The reason is that, without patterns, colours and textures become more important and, unlike what happens with patterns, designers have not thought out beforehand how to mix them. Take the neutral palette first – not, of course, that neutrals are always so indeterminate that they sink into the background (think of

ABOVE This is a highly sophisticated scheme that matches the subtlest shades of grey and off-white with bland steel furniture and the neutrals of blond wood and canework. The textures in the room come from the natural wood and willow.
ABOVE RIGHT The cream and white linens covering the sofas match the vellum on the drawing-room wall. Everything is restrained except for the two cushions, whose inclusion draws each element together.
RIGHT Fashion fabrics from Donegal, including linens and tweeds, have been used to make throws, cushions and covers for an elegant Parisian sitting room.

the pairing of black and white, for example). But imagine the rarified combinations of string, bone and stone: use them in textured wool or cashmere, as throws, cushions and curtains, and you have a look, urban and sybaritic, that adds luxury to comfort. Put those same off-white shades into cotton and create echoes of the scraped-bone colours of the seaside home, the suggestion of seafood picnics on the sand and long summer nights on the verandah. In silk, the same shades will say exactly the opposite, especially if you change the textures from slub and loose-weave fabrics to satin, matt silks and bias-cut glamour. In silk, the off-whites scream Syrie Maugham, the extravagant and luxurious 1930s.

ABOVE Choosing a neutral colour scheme gives you the opportunity to experiment with textures, as in this comfortable but unassuming guest bedroom. A Durham quilt contrasts with a waffle coverlet; taupe blankets catch the colour of the matting. The whole effect is restrained and utterly simple.

LEFT A series of natural colours in beige and cream are teamed together for this autumnal group. The interest lies in the varied textures, from herringbone to nubbly weaves, as much as the colours.

It was not until the 20th century that the understated virtues of neutral shades became smart. This was because fashion, whether in clothes or furnishings, tends to veer to the most expensive objects available. Before the invention of aniline dyes in the 19th century, it was a long and tedious process to colour fabrics; this was true even of monochromes such as toile de Jouy. And, before the invention of powered looms and Jacquard weaving, most patterned fabrics had to be woven by hand. As a result, the cheapest – and least sought after – fabrics were the plain weaves of a single colour.

Fashion also reacts to what has gone before. When multicoloured chintzes and woven paisleys were available to the middle classes, the smart folk started looking towards neutrals, especially pale-coloured ones that were expensive to clean and maintain. This was why Syrie Maugham hit the spot when the generation that followed the First World War reacted to the grotesque over-stuffing and over-furnishing that saw out the 19th century and the extravagance of the Edwardian era that followed it.

Our current longing for the the neutral and the natural is a similar reaction against the vulgarity of the 1980s and the way the world is being taken over by industrial processes. We long for handwoven fabrics with

visible faults, for yarns coloured with vegetable dyes and for a lack of pattern compensated by an interest in texture. Neutrals are far from easy to get right. Look at the trade cards issued by paint firms and you will see the huge variations to be found in cream and beige alone. While any cream looks good with any white or black, few creams will look good together.

LEFT Clever mixing of different kinds of leather enhances the effects of each. Here plain dark suede is contrasted with brown overstitched suede and the softest glove leather. The colours are all shades of taupe and brown.
ABOVE No easy chair is easier on the eye – and the bum – than a leather-upholstered club armchair. The more you sit in it the better it gets. This stylish version has a matching tan suede cushion made of irregular patchwork.
RIGHT Loose covers for the sofa and pouffe are in a natural cotton; interest comes from the soft cashmere cushions and neutral, earthy throw.

It's a question of the quantity of red tones in the colours. The same applies to the mid tones of grey or beige, while even white and black, which would seem safe together, can have wide variations.

Texture adds a further complication in that the whorls and ribs, patterns and slubs will catch and hold the light and the reflections from the fabrics around them. Try putting a piece of creamy Donegal tweed alongside red felt and you will appreciate how carefully neutrals need to be positioned.

The simplest solution is to start with a swatch board for all the possible fabrics, from curtains to cushions to rugs, and add to that the shades you plan for walls, ceiling, floor and furniture. You can take advantage of the way light shades react to primary colours by actually encouraging the reflections of one on another while also subtly revealing the intricacies of plain white.

Combining neutrals also needs a good deal of skill because some mixtures – think coffee and cream – are utterly dated to the 1970s, although no doubt they will eventually enjoy a comeback. Yet coffee can currently be happily allied with black or terracotta, while cream is being teamed with whites and beiges. A neutral scheme is therefore difficult to achieve but is highly adaptable when you get it right.

LEFT AND ABOVE Neutrals don't have to be boring. The sofa shown left is made welcoming in this grey-walled living room by being a touch pinker than the rest of the scheme. The warm tones of the wood cupboards also make for friendliness. Cushions on the sofa opposite (shown above) bring together the room's greys and off-whites without shouting about their intention.

RIGHT Grey, like black and white, comes in all sorts of shades – bluer, pinker, browner. When you are matching fabrics to furniture, check that the shades complement each other. But don't bother to get an exact match.

FAR LEFT Ribbon makes a decorative feature on two plain blankets. It is threaded through the loose mohair weave of the top one and used as a hem for the conventional wool version.
CENTRE LEFT This is a clever way of using the charms of wool and tweed. The chair is covered in a fuchsia Donegal tweed, which turns up as patchwork and piping on a pink herringbone cushion. The brilliant raspberry throw gives extra oomph.
NEAR LEFT Interest in green issues has led to a longing for natural colours and textures such as this roughly woven earth-coloured blanket of wool.
BELOW Wool dyes well in shades of orange, beige and brown, and this chair shows how harmoniously they mix. Herringbone tweeds are bordered in neutral shades and complemented by a tweed patchwork cushion.

wools and velvets

Of all the fabrics available to the 21st-century designer, wools and velvets come with the greatest weight of history. Fragments of woven wool have turned up in Babylonian graves; in the House of Lords the Lord Chancellor sits on a sack of wool to remind Britain that wool was responsible for its rise to power; and the paintings of the Renaissance are heavy with the richness of silk velvet, cut into patterns that are still available in Italy today.

Wool is one of the most adaptable fabrics. Depending on the breed of sheep – or, I suppose, goat, llama or alpaca – the textile that results can either be tough enough to be woven into a pile-free Scottish tweed carpet (a tradition recently revived by the Highland firm of Anta) or fine enough to be knitted into a baby's christening shawl that will, like silk, run through a wedding ring. Wool can be dyed in the brightest colours or left in the original colour of the fleece – anything from off-white to dusky grey or dark brown. Its weave can vary from the outbreaks of Donegal tweed, whose porridgy texture is enlivened with random spots of primary colours, to the smoothest, sheeniest worsted made from 100 per cent superfine wool.

Through the centuries wool has given the world classic fabrics: tweed and tartan from Scotland, now copied from Japan to Milan; paisleys from India, which arrived as cashmere shawls and became a Victorian craze that never went away; kilims from Persia, Afghanistan and dozens of wandering Middle Eastern tribes that recently moved away from carpets to become hangings, cushions, covers for sofas and chairs, luggage and even slippers. Flannels, worsted and pinstripes covered generations of business bottoms and gangster shoulder pads before moving into curtains and beds, while knitted wool in all its traditional modes, from Fair Isle to Guernsey, is the inspiration behind dozens of fabric textures and patterns.

Its uses in rooms are just as various. Interior designers such as John Stefanides have taken updates of tattersalls (more often found on racing men's waistcoats) and tweeds to make fine sofa covers; the architect

THIS PAGE Tweeds were originally intended to blend with the mountains, and this lovely autumnal mix catches the flaring woods and brackens of Ireland, where all these woollens were woven. Being rugged by nature, tweeds will stand any amount of mixing and matching.

RIGHT An effective mingling of fabrics for a chair: the soft purple upholstery is made of velvet, while the generous cushion is in silk with a more robust cotton trim.

OPPOSITE PAGE The room continues the effective mixture of textures and fabrics with a leather stool at its centre, a large L-shaped sofa in neutral grey cotton and subtle cushions in silk. The floor cushions are made of stronger cotton.

Sophie Hicks delights in using grey flannel to drape long Georgian windows in London houses; while Tessa Kennedy does outrageous things with multicoloured tartans. The secret is to do the unexpected. A Fair Isle sweater could embrace a tubby chair; a blue chalk stripe would make a fine bedspread; and the discreet ribs of fishermen's jerseys just plead to be cushion covers. Harris tweed is so tough that it could cope with a troupe of performing circus dogs jumping on it, while the subtle checks and stripes of Scottish estate tweeds just ask to be mixed together as curtains, covers, cushions and carpets.

Other European countries do use wool – I recently came across a thick teased weave made in the mountains of Tuscany to wrap round chilled shepherds in winter – but it is hard to think of any nation that has made such good use of its sheep as Britain. The Lord Chancellor's Woolsack is there by right.

If woven wool is a British triumph, then velvet must belong to the Italians. There are shops in Florence where the gorgeous complexities of 14th-century design, the curves and swirls, the cutting and shearing, the dyeing and weaving, can still be found, where velvet is made on ancient machines according to ancient secrets. Velvets, especially silk velvet, whose raised pile can be stroked like a cat's fur, were the aristocrats of the world of fabrics. Modern techniques may mean that their richness has been superseded by that of suede and cashmere, and their current unfashionableness has deprived most people of the chance to experience the glamour of a beautiful velvet, but decorators such as Alidad, whose Eastern roots enable him to appreciate velvet's allure, are slowly returning to its charms.

The aim should be to use velvet – or, for that matter, tartan or flannel – in unexpected ways and in unexpected colours. Velvet is, of course, plain-coloured. Its variations come from self-coloured patterns, cutting the pile to different lengths, or varying areas of pile with areas of plain, gleaming silk. The furry pile and the naked silk provide such a contrast of textures that there is no need for other shades or colours. The most extreme example of this is devoré, which made a comeback a few years ago, firstly as fashion wraps but latterly as throws. Here the silk pile is complemented by silk so fine that it is a

sheer chiffon; the idea is that, when draped and folded, the patterns should be endlessly repeated and refined through the transparent veils. But its uses are limited by its fragility. An uncut silk velvet can survive for generations; cut, the fabric becomes ever more delicate, though well-treated silk can survive where wool will not.

Once the cutting reaches its extremes, as in devoré, it will survive only as pure decoration. Use it as a throw on an unused chair, a drape over a chaise longue in a boudoir or for the hangings of a four-poster bed. Consider cut velvet, too, as a background for a fine oil painting. The Old Masters knew what they were doing when they placed their Virgins and their saints against backdrops of velvet for its sheen attracts the light and, with it, attention. But, if your velvet is in the premier league, the picture must be too.

LEFT Velvets, such as this operatic swagger of dark green, work well in night-time rooms and in winter. In this room, they can simply be removed on sunnier days.
BELOW Silk is exceptionally good at taking dyes and, when made into velvet, elegantly catches textures and sheen. All these properties have been used for this tab-hung curtain.
OPPOSITE PAGE, LEFT The luxurious silk and velvet cushions in this understated room have been deliberately chosen to enhance the modern abstract painting.

OPPOSITE PAGE, ABOVE RIGHT Cushion covers don't need to be of a single fabric. Here silk and velvet are joined with a single line of piping.
OPPOSITE PAGE, BELOW RIGHT Velvet comes in all sorts of stylish patterns and textures. The top cushion on the pile is harlequin velvet with fancy tassels; the one below is of velvet cut in a traditional damask pattern.

faux furs, suedes and leathers

Real furs, such as the bear skins mounded up on the bed of Ivan the Terrible in old Hollywood movies, are clearly politically incorrect in modern interiors. Whether the animals they came from were trapped or farmed, pelts used in soft furnishings are generally unacceptable to 21st-century humans. But we can't, it seems, do without the approximation of fur. We need the soft security of deep grey chinchilla for our bare feet to play in and the velvety texture of beaver to smooth in our laps. Nor can we relinquish the colours, the camouflage, the patterns that nature gave.

We now revel in faux furs, artfully teased from artificial fabrics and patterned as though the shy Polydamide once strolled across Africa's veldt, hiding itself from predators by evolving a synthetic fur striped and barred like strong sunlight against the trees. Even in its new, manmade mode, fur remains as exotic as when 20th-century design luminaries such as Diana Vreeland and Cecil Beaton, Valentino and Le Corbusier used real pelts, from leopard to pony, for their carpets, cushions and chairs. Recently, designers of the suites of London's grandest hotels have upholstered chairs in mock zebra and bordered bedspreads with cheating cheetah – and the aura these rooms evoke is that of a banquet about to begin.

Pelts from exotic animals, hunted among the high deserts of Africa or the dripping forests of Sumatra, have been synonymous with forbidden luxury since the Romans lounged on couches bedecked with lion skins. Even though we have now substituted coal derivatives for the real thing, we have still not got rid of the baggage which goes with tawny stripes.

But this is luxury to be found for not much cost. The new faux furs perform much better than the old skins. They are easily worked by the upholsterer; they can be cleaned if you tip your lunch over them; they evoke no pain-filled animal deaths – and they don't suffer from moth. Better still, you can upholster a set of chairs, whether dining, office or armchairs, in a mix of animals. One can be cheetah, another leopard, a third tiger, along with zebra, giraffe or ocelot; because all take their colours from nature – a mixture of black, browns, fawns and creams – they will all complement each other, especially if you buy different fabrics from the same maker.

Don't confine your use of faux furs to upholstery. Suitably backed, the less hairy faux furs make great throws or even curtains. Real skins tended to be backed with a plain felt, from black to scarlet, and this makes a good foil for fakes too. Hairier fakes, such as bear, wolf and monkey, work less well for pure upholstery – well, they won't work at all – but are fine in throws, scatter rugs and cushions. Think Ivan the Terrible and pile them on your bed.

OPPOSITE PAGE, ABOVE Leather is best used to upholster versions of the club armchair. It can add an element of luxury which is either traditional or, as here, modernist in essence.

OPPOSITE PAGE, BELOW Leather does not have to be brown or black. New ways of colouring the hides mean that soft neutrals can be used in upholstery.

BELOW Hide is one of the longest lasting upholstery materials, which actually improves with wear. It is perfect for these kitchen stools since it can be easily wiped down.

TOP RIGHT Interiors have recently been inspired by smart luggage. These leather door handles are clearly influenced by Vuitton trunks.

CENTRE RIGHT One conspicuous disadvantage of leather is that it has a slithery feel. But the problem can be solved by allying it with a textured velvet.

BOTTOM RIGHT Leather is increasingly being used for accessories – as in this practical storage bin. Generally, it works best in natural colours.

In a glossy fashion magazine I recently saw a pair of fishing trousers: they were of the palest stone suede, beautifully tailored and costing around £1000. Perfect for fishing, enthused the editor – as long as you didn't get a spot of damp on them. This is the point of suede: it is beautiful, comfortable, luxurious, expensive and extremely impractical. And that is why we love it

more substantial. Used in the way Amberg favours – in darkish natural colours, severely cut into squares and rectangles and sewn together – its message is masculine. It somehow recalls the interiors of private jets and luxury cars, state rooms in 1930s transatlantic liners and briefcases teamed with cashmere coats. Leather epitomizes the great age of travel and, used

LEFT An earthy brown suede cushion tops a pile of throws where both colours and textures have been carefully chosen.

RIGHT Even a tiny amount of suede or leather adds a touch of luxury. The plain cotton curtains are held back with a pair of soft brown suede and leather ties.

OPPOSITE PAGE, CLOCKWISE FROM TOP LEFT
A subtle mixture of textures characterizes this seat. The chair is in suede with a ponyskin cushion at the back and a soft woollen throw over all.

A plain armchair has been closely covered in the palest suede to emphasize its strong outline.

This scheme makes use of realistic faux ponyskin for the easy chairs and places them formally on a fake fur rug.

A fake giraffe fabric has been used to cover everything on this X-stool, even the legs. It is placed at the bottom of a bed in similar colours.

around the house. Since the days of Jean Harlow, the palest matt skins have been used to cover beds, sofas and cushions and, while advances in curing and protecting the skins have made suede a teeny bit more practical, no one could say that it was sensible to have it around young children, animals or even those liable to spill their Ribena in a fit of absentmindedness.

While suede comes from the inside of the skin, leather comes from the outside, which makes it capable of coping with rather more; it has a shiny, slightly more impervious topside than the nap of suede, which sucks up liquids like blotting paper.

Leather has been making a serious comeback lately – not just for upholstery (where it has been used ever since upholstery was invented) but also for floors, walls and furniture such as tables and consoles. A leading exponent in this area is Bill Amberg, who was first known for his handbags but then became more ambitious.

Leather was extensively used instead of wallpaper in 17th-century Europe. Most commonly originating in Spain, it was embossed, blind-stamped and burnished to create the sort of baroque patterns that now turn up on damask. Since quite a lot of it is still around, leather obviously has lasting qualities. However, whereas suede around the house implies modernity, money and even minimalism, leather stands for something

in the modern style, can evoke associations with first-class cabins and Pullman sleepers along with Art Deco curves and colours recently revived by Connolly, which provides leather for Rolls Royce's classier cars. You can also use it to reinvent 17th-century interiors, where it can perform the same service as tapestries or panelling: reducing draughts, adding insulation and improving acoustics, while looking dourly decorative.

New techniques for curing hides seem to have brought both suede and leather down in price and the sizes of skins available are, for some reason, more generous than before. This allows you to upholster quite large areas without obtrusive seams. Do not be wooed into using leather in random pieces for patchwork. It is always obvious that crazy patchworking is a cheap solution that uses up the left-over bits from more important jobs.

Whatever you do with it, leather is a sombre covering that will add weight to a room, while suede somehow suggests frivolity. If we were allowed to be sexist, we would admit that leather is masculine in tone and suede is feminine. And, I suppose, the most recent introduction into the plain, skinny range – manmade fleece – is animal.

Manmade fleece has none of the problems of suede or leather. It can even be tossed into a washing machine when the kids drop pizza all over it. It is satisfyingly cuddlable – but, no, it will never have an aura of luxury.

checks, stripes and geometrics

Checks and stripes have had a huge renaissance in the past few years, which means that they may soon become passé. If you don't care about fashion, take no notice of this – for they will surely come around again. If you do care, use checked and striped fabrics in new and unusual mixtures and colours to bring them back to life.

TOP Woven fabric makes up the chair back and seat, which is echoed by the striped drugget on the floor and the checked cushions on the nearby sofa. The simplicity works for an office-cum-living room.
ABOVE A bold gingham wall covering in red and white backs a brilliant yellow wall cupboard full of red and white pottery. It is surprisingly easy to match country reds and yellows with each other.
RIGHT The 17th-century panelling of a Scandinavian sitting room is matched by the checks and stripes of the sofa's bolsters and loose cover and the chair cushion. Even the rug takes up the scheme.
FAR RIGHT Nothing could be more out of date than traditional net curtains. If you need to be screened from the road, consider the charms of checked voile.

ABOVE LEFT Star shapes are good fun, especially in a seaside setting, but they are difficult to make and stuff. Use a simple checked fabric.
ABOVE CENTRE This cushion's dark green bobbled border is several tones deeper than the colours of the stripes.
ABOVE RIGHT There are four different checks in this lively scheme, plus both blue and sage green. It works because, along with plain areas of colour, each check has the same off-white background.
LEFT These striped café-style curtains have no gathering and are held up by tabs.

A few years ago, one of the best forecasters in the interior design world was asked what the next big thing in fabrics would be. 'Checks,' she snapped back without hesitation – and so it proved. You couldn't get away from checks, especially the simple gingham ones, generally in a single primary colour and off-white. Houses were bedecked with red and white checks: curtains, tablecloths, upholstery, cushions, bedspreads and even rugs were covered with little squares. Stripes in the same cottons and colours were running a close second.

Predictably, everything has changed. All-over gingham now looks as old-hat as Laura Ashley's tiny flowers or gigantic blowsy roses on English chintz. These basic patterns, however, never go away – they never have since the earliest weavers discovered how to create strips of different colours just by varying the warp and weft. If a gingham or plain stripe is rather boring – both are achieved by regular, all-square variations – stripes and

OPPOSITE PAGE Linings in the 18th century were often patterned with checks and stripes, as exemplified in this French interior. The pretty floral stripe is used for both walls and sofa, while the red gingham – picking up on a colour from the floral stripe – makes up undercurtains and other upholstery.

checks are certainly not. To be inspired, I have only to think of the Regency stripe, in subtle or dramatic colours such as slate grey and dark purple, sage and black, or blue and turquoise. Add to this a lustrous fabric such as silk rep or matt and satin silks – and you have fabrics that are little short of palatial. Stripes can also be achieved by techniques such as teaming cut and uncut velvet in the same colour. Stripes that vary in width and colour, as in the superior French tickings, soft Swedish stripes within stripes and Ian Mankin's clever modern tickings all have a fine 18th-century look which, because it is essentially unfussy, suits modern interiors as well as 18th-century town houses extremely well.

For some reason, stripes evoke the town and checks evoke the country. While there are silk checks to be had – ones which conjure up the black and white *Vogue* Regency look of the 1930s, as well as brilliant Thai silks and glowing reworks of traditional tartans – lush checks are relatively rare.

Checks in cotton or linen abound and, given plenty of bulk with a good lining and backing, form heavyweight curtains and upholstery good enough for a country house as well as a country cottage. The simplicity of the pattern means that they can also be adapted to suit modernist architecture – and even to satisfy minimalists who want curtains or blinds to shield them from their neighbours and cut out the daylight. My own favourites in the check and stripe line are the handwoven French fabrics that were used in the 18th and

19th centuries to provide cheaper backs to pictorial toiles – each check in these is quite large, about 4–5cm (1½–2in) square, and in simple (but often unexpected) colours. If the fabric is genuinely old, the dyes will be made from vegetables, which gives an added softness to the already homespun weave from the handloom.

I have a fine Nîmes check (Nîmes was the origin of denim, a corruption of *de Nîmes*) in dark indigo and rose madder and others of the same size which vary the rose or navy with a dull white. All three can, of course, be teamed together because the vegetable dyes are all roughly the same shade. Add to these the splendid French featherproof tickings – far more varied and convincing, and still to be found covering bolsters and mattresses in hotels all over France and even on sleeper trains – and you have a rich source of country decor. I recently bought a length of cotton, woven in pale greige with a brilliant orange stripe at the edges, which I shall use to make bathroom curtains. It was originally intended for roller towels.

ABOVE A greige and off-white checked cotton is padded and fixed onto the walls. The same fabric is used for the curtains, while the blind has a pretty lace trim.
RIGHT The cupboards in the bedroom have been given the same treatment as the walls, with the gingham fabric stretched over the doors and an ornamental dado below it.

THIS PAGE Subtle silks in neutral shades cover both the sofa and large stools in this serene sitting room – in which everything is subsidiary to the modern sculpture. The silks are all washable.

LEFT AND BELOW Shades of the 1950s
are evident in this 'contemporary' chair,
which has been covered in figured
wool. The same 'cubist' pattern is
repeated in the cushion, where the
pattern has actually been stitched
onto the cotton cover.

If you enjoy working with checks and stripes, antique shops specializing in textiles are a rich source of finds, particularly because the colourways are so unexpected. But modern colourists are working with heavy cottons woven in the East to produce fabrics in equally soft sages, pinks and terracottas – especially Ian Mankin, the tsar of ticking.

The advantage of new fabrics – apart from their relative cheapness and the fact that they recognize washing machines – is that the dyes used for different widths and variations of checks and stripes are the same. This means that, with skill, you can add a striped loose cover to an old chair, edge it with cord covered in the colour of the stripe and pile it high with cushions in all sorts of checks but still in the same shade. Beware of being too clever: think how contrived a woman looks if her dress, shoes, bag and brooch all match. It's fine to have terracotta covers and cushions as long as you add in the odd wild card such as a flowery chintz with minimal touches of terracotta among the pinks and greens.

Matching fabrics is one of the skills for which designers are paid. I recently toured every single suite in four of the grandest London hotels, where names such as John Stefanides, Nina Campbell and Tessa Kennedy had been hired to give each apartment an air of luxurious individuality. Combinations such as tweeds with tattersall checks and Donegal slubs were used on the cushions and sofas and behind wardrobe grilles to provide a soothing softness which was none the less both luxurious and urban in its effect – a room to return to after a tiring day. Elsewhere silk

tartans had been swathed over coronas of double beds and one of their shades had been picked up by an equally costly lining, while the same tartan in a woven wool might be contrasted with plainer checks and stripes of the same colours in the living room.

The point about checks and stripes is that you can bend them to your will. They make fewer statements than, say, a brocade or floral; they are more easily sewn than large and ornate patterns; and, unlike plains, they provide a helpful variation of shade and tone. My forecaster was right to pinpoint the coming craze but the truth is that these plainest of all patterns have never gone away since weaving was invented.

OPPOSITE PAGE A Swedish-style room in Connecticut has bland chairs, walls and a painted chequerboard floor. It has been given a lift by three brightly coloured flowery cushions.

LEFT The fabric used to cover the cushions is a cotton piped in lime green. The pattern has deliberately been overscaled to create a bold and dramatic effect that is well suited to a large room.

BELOW In the 18th century, dining chairs were put around the walls when not in use. Here three have been casually placed around a plain white table. The room's restrained decor is highly effective.

the new florals

Many of the new florals are actually old florals that had fallen out of fashion. These are the fabrics of the early 20th century: full of roses and fuchsias, ivies and geraniums printed in crisp colours on neutral grounds. Used in the modern idiom, they have a freshness that is appealing in both rural and urban schemes.

I used to get the feeling that every middle-class living room in England (not Britain) was covered in yards and yards of floral chintz. If this fashion had been spearheaded by anyone but an accountant, it was hard to think who. Each background was dirty white or mud in colour and on it were flowers chosen for their hideous shapes. These were generally coloured in sludge brown and corset pink with luridly green leaves curling around the horrid blooms. Often the lady of the house had, over the years, sewn her own tapestries for footstools and chairs in similar shades. (Except one aristocratic couple I came across: she did the exciting bits of dirty brown flower and lurid leaf; he, when not otherwise occupied at the House of Lords, was condemned to the slavery of the backgrounds.)

However, starting with the blessed John Fowler, good taste gradually appeared in these depressing drawing rooms. It has taken half a century, but now those ugly linen unions have been confined to the dustbin of decor (though they will probably make a retro comeback in the near future). The designer Cath Kidston has already revived the prettier rosebud prints of the mid 20th century. They appear on laundry bags and padded coathangers, lampshades and filing boxes – and she wears them as dresses, combined with brown lisle-lookalike stockings.

RIGHT A traditional floral chintz is surprisingly at home in a modern scheme. While everything else is very 20th century, the fabric is 19th – chosen for its clean lines and unsullied use of colour.

Fowler's chintzes, which look as stylish to the 21st-century eye as when he produced them in the 1950s, were very frequently reworked from 18th-century fabrics. Berkeley Sprig came from a wallpaper discovered behind old damask in Berkeley Square and, before that, had probably been inspired by a 17th-century embroidered quilt; the firm later adopted Berkeley Sprig as its logo. Ledbury came from the lining of a 19th-century German box. Passion Flower – a strong design that alternates flowers in urns on an ultramarine background with strawberries and hunting dogs – was inspired by a Regency fabric.

All modern floral designers search for such original documents – which are as likely to relate to 18th-century silk dresses as to furnishing fabrics. Laura Ashley notably found her miniature flower sprigs among the fabric swatches at the Victoria and Albert Museum, while Geoffrey Bennison

ABOVE Traditional floral patterns can, when overscaled, look totally modern. This cushion gives the room its only splash of colour.
RIGHT Now that designers have caught on to the charms of 19th-century cottons, styles similar to this flowery chintz should be easy to find.

THIS PAGE The same floral, stripy fabric has been used for the cotton blind and the large bed cushion. Different fabrics in the same theme turn up in the quilt, the unusual chair and even in a little storage basket. Sensibly, the curtains are a plain white voile.

RIGHT A little bit of pretty fabric can go a long way in a simple bedroom. This floral coverlet barely covers the sheet, but that doesn't matter. Adding matching but real flowers nearby is a neat touch.
BELOW Junk shops, flea markets and car boot sales can be excellent sources of undervalued linens. Seek out hemstitched sheets, as shown here, and softly old-fashioned florals.

was so determined to replicate the antique feeling of his subfusc florals that he set many of them on a background of soft brown – a colour achieved by staining white fabric with strong tea.

Today there is a more deliberate cross-fertilization between fashion and furnishing fabric than ever before. The lace, velvet and devoré that mingled with the teensy roses and braided cardigans of *fin de siècle* fashions were originally more at home on tablecloths, tatted guest towels and bedspreads than in the nightclub. Tartans jumped from kilts to carpets in the 19th century but, in this, they were joined by floral chintz in the Italian designs of Etro and in Nina Campbell's and Tessa Kennedy's 'faux' Scottish rooms. From the Indian chintzes which came to Britain via Marseilles in the 17th century – much to the delight of the wife of diarist Samuel Pepys – we rediscovered a love affair with the Provençal floral prints of Souleiado.

Where new florals differ from the old drawing-room drab is in their scale and colouring. Colefax and Fowler florals stand brightly on fresh white or figured backgrounds and are not afraid of using strong colours. Fowler also liked to change the scales of the early fabrics he discovered: a tiny print used in the 18th century as a drawer lining might reappear boldly oversized and sharpened in colour. Other patterns might diminish until the overall look was little more than groupings of dots. As with all fabrics, the skill in working with florals lies in doing the unexpected. This is not easy because

the unexpected is constantly being done – and becoming jaded in the process. Florals with tartan have more or less had their day, while the technique of treating flowers as botanic prints on strong, plain backgrounds needs to be carefully confined to a single use per room. The swags and ruches of the 1980s (originally dreamt up by John Fowler, who had been inspired by a bustled 19th-century ballgown) will probably not see the light of day again for decades, but before long there is certain to be a revival of floral prints teamed with strong but unusual plain colours, and flowers with leopard or tiger skin are here and now. There's plenty more mileage in teaming flowery fabrics with complementary checks and stripes and bringing together contrasting fabrics such as floral printed voile and gossamer-fine wool or tweed and linen.

The way to get it right is to follow the example of Fowler himself. The colour board may be a hoary old tool in the decorator's workshop – but it's there because it works.

If your intention is to create a floral room that is reminiscent of the countryside and the rose garden, a floral fabric should be the dominant element in the furnishing scheme. So pick a juicy one, well designed and cleverly coloured. Make this the background of your board and add to it the braids, the papers, the tweeds and lawns that you think will produce the effect you are trying to achieve.

For such details as piping on cushions, I find that it is always a good idea to pick one strong or dark shade – a forest green, for instance – that is already in the material along with a neutral colour plus one other really pretty colour from the original fabric. Don't be tempted to pick too many shades, however, or you will end up with an overall effect that is fragmentary or too clever by half. After a few days' contemplation, you will discover if you have made the right decision.

ABOVE LEFT A pretty floral fabric may have more uses than you think. Don't simply consign it to the cottage and the Victorian terrace, but put it in a modern kitchen or bathroom, for instance.
FAR LEFT Experiment with different combinations of fabrics. This pink print has nothing obviously in common with the multicoloured floral, but they work together in a plain off-white room.
LEFT Only recently have we come to value old-fashioned florals for more than their nostalgic charm. They are enjoying a high fashion revival both in the home and on the clothes rack.

silks and damasks

These fabrics are the aristocrats of the fabric world and correspondingly expensive. Used in quantity, they have enormous grandeur and must be carefully treated. In smaller amounts, the fabrics' ability to take dyes will result in touches of brilliant colour. Since damasks have monochrome patterns woven in, different designs in the same shade can be combined, as can similar patterns in different shades.

LEFT The sophistication of these chairs means that they could only be French. They are upholstered in similar, though not identical, damask patterns in different rich shades, while the heavy bullion fringe binds the colours together.
ABOVE RIGHT One of the rich autumnal colours used in this elegant silk-damask cushion appears in a deeper tone in the chair underneath. Such expensive fabrics don't break the bank when they are used for cushion covers only.
OPPOSITE PAGE A grand hotel drawing room – the home of the same French chairs – demonstrates how to mix and mingle silk damask's colours, patterns and elegance with an unswervingly sure touch.

Without doubt, silks and damasks are the aristocrats of the fabric world. The Chinese invented the spinning of silk from the cocoon of the silk worm early in their history, while the word 'damask' comes from the Syrian city of Damascus – and the self-patterned fabric probably arrived in western Europe as a result of the Crusades.

Despite its softness and fragility, silk is remarkably resistant – and does not suffer from moth. Thus a crimson Italian silk damask ordered by King William III in 1689 for a presence chamber in the palace at Hampton Court did not need to be replaced until 1923. Even then, the silk was accurately copied.

The method of weaving and the ornate patterns so typical of silk damask have also survived. National Trust houses in Britain and the great châteaux of France regularly replace their 17th- and 18th-century hangings – for this fabric has always been used as a wall covering as well as for soft furnishings – and curtains with damasks that are woven in exactly the same way they were 500 years ago. Some specialist firms go as far as to use the old-fashioned vegetable dyes as well.

However grand, silk damasks have to be used with care. Their sumptuous looks can too easily turn into the kind of grandiose flock-wallpaper effect familiar from old-fashioned steak houses and Indian restaurants. Crimson is particularly difficult – and I suggest that you really need palatial surroundings and equivalent furniture and pictures before you risk it. The other colours are easier: ultramarine and midnight blue are grand but more unexpected. (They

RIGHT In a damask fabric the pattern is merely hinted at in the weave. Damask is perfect for upholstery in grand but understated rooms.

FAR RIGHT Woven fabrics, such as this traditionally patterned curtain, can be left unlined because the pattern is visible, though reversed, from both sides. Allow the light to pick up the complexities of the damask weave.

BELOW Although it has to compete with modern paintings and abstract lights, this antique upholstered chair is still the star of the set with its authentic 18th-century print fabric.

would look fine in the sort of Georgian houses found in British cities such as London, Bath and Edinburgh and, of course, in Italian palazzi or the town houses of Paris and New York.) Damask in soft khaki is even more adaptable, as are the off-whites.

Silk damasks work even better (and are just about affordable) when used in very small quantities. The decorator Emily Todhunter, a practical soul, has pioneered the idea of handkerchief-sized damasks, and other expensive textiles, patchworked onto cushion covers, while grander schemes use small rectanagles of fabrics to hang behind good-quality oil paintings. Such an effect can turn an average landscape into an Old Master. Teamed with tweeds or tartans or silky stripes, the richness of damask adds stability and depth of colour.

Silk – textured, intricately woven in herringbones or chequers, left with bobbly slubs or striped in brilliant colours – provides a strong look in many urban schemes. (It is often too strong for the country except in a really grand interior.) The brilliance and constrasts of Thai silk are splendid for the kind of eclectic scheme often found in American city interiors, where it is ideal with Chinese porcelain, oriental rugs and Japanese gold-backed screens; so are plain but textured silks.

I love the idea of a city scheme worked around a whole series of whites and off-whites with textures from satin smooth to near-chunky silk tweed. Try this in a loft or warehouse space. Let it add a touch of luxury to a minimalist apartment – and improve the harsh acoustics that minimalism often encourages.

Although silks were made all over Europe from the Renaissance onwards, they still retain their oriental roots except when, like traditional damasks, the patterns come from an entirely different tradition. Embroidered Chinese silks, with paeonies and butterflies sewn on in satin stitch, the gold-laced fabrics covered with rank badges for ascending mandarins, and silks painted with scenes of tumbling children are still both easily available and relatively good value. Something a bit simpler would be more appropriate for curtains, but consider these colourful and busy fabrics for cushions, for hangings, for small bags – even displayed under glass in a tray or table.

But do keep away from crimson.

ABOVE Taupe, cerulean blue and soft lime-green raw silks are sewn together for cushion and bolster covers on a large L-shaped sofa.
OPPOSITE PAGE, BOTTOM RIGHT Small touches, such as this cushion covered in a rich oriental-type brocade, can dictate the style of a room. In this case, East meets West.

pictorials and toiles

Of all the textiles used for decorating, the pictorials are by far the most fun. They include the toiles, from Jouy and other French factories (though illustrated cottons were just as fashionable in England in the latter half of the 18th century), the more robust chintzes that arrived from India in the 17th century and some modern classics such as Timney and Fowler's designs culled from black and white illustrations – anything from caesars' heads to blue whales – exotic animals found on Andrew Martin's upholstery fabrics and the painted designs, using calligraphy and gilded damask swirls, created by textile innovators such as Caroline Quartermaine and Neil Bottle.

ABOVE LEFT Toile de Jouy patterns can be extremely robust and with a huge repeat. Take advantage of this by cutting out a single motif to use on a chair seat.
ABOVE RIGHT The same pattern reappears as the central motif for the bedhead and for the quilt on the bed itself. The room's walls have a matching fabric stripe, while curtains and cushions incorporate a check in the same colour.
OPPOSITE PAGE The French often use fabric instead of paper on the walls, especially when the room has a dado. This 18th-century authentic toile of Arcadian scenes is used for everything – but the room survives because of its plain dado and floor.

Pictorial designs are as old as decorating itself. Think of the huge tapestries used to help the acoustics and minimize the draughts in stone castles such as the Tower of London. Great expanses would be given over to the doings of the classical gods: rape and assassination, war and peace were all depicted in colours much more gaudy than they now seem. The bright yellows and reds have faded to give tapestries their distinctive bluish-green looks – but they are still a great way of making an old house cosier. At the

tapestry edges can be found charming details such as elephants and spouting fish, marvellous seashells on exotic beaches and bouquets of pretty flowers. It is these afterthoughts that have come to dominate pictorial fabrics from the 18th-century toiles de Jouy onwards.

A later toile, with a sidelong hurray at Napoleon's 1805 campaign in Egypt, restricted itself to pyramids and sphinxes without any symbols of victory, while others showed farmyard scenes, the complex dyeing of toile itself and lovers in Arcadia. Toiles in America glorified the country's buildings. the lives of George Washington and Benjamin Franklin (accompanied by Liberty and Minerva, in grand old tapestry tradition), while English toiles from Manchester boasted of the empire, the far-flung lands and the quaint costumes of Wales and Scotland.

Victorian grandeur led to some absurdly printed fabrics with false swags, lace effects and pseudo gilding – until William Morris and Art Nouveau designers created their own pictorial effects of birds in foliage, wreathed grapes and vine leaves along with more obvious florals. These enjoyed a tremendous comeback in the 1960s, when old printing plates were dusted down and, all too often, scaled down or otherwise spoilt.

ABOVE In classical schemes the patterned fabric made up the main curtain while the inner curtain consisted of a plain, checked or striped fabric. In this room the classical style is reversed to great effect. The chair is covered with the same chintz.

LEFT A complex pattern such as a toile de Jouy may require a border to delineate the curtain's shape – as shown in this example. Similarly, goblet pleats allow the fabric to speak for itself.

RIGHT The pretty toile de Jouy upholstery of an unpretentious tub chair is enlivened with a crimson tasselled border, which gives it extra pzazz.

OPPOSITE PAGE Monochrome schemes – especially in black and white – are very much of today. This one is extremely clever, with the curtain border matching the walls while the chair's pattern is entirely different.

RIGHT Old quilts are not always patchwork. English-made ones often used a single monochrome fabric that was then quilted over, regardless of pattern. The colours of this fine example are matched in the other furnishings.
BELOW A decorative blue toile de Jouy has been given a bobbly edge in contrasting red. The red shade is picked up in the striped chair and in the antique basket which sits on it.

From the end of the 19th century, decorating stopped being so jolly with, at best, the vorticist designs of the 1920s and 1930s and, at worst (if you like a good pictorial fabric) the all-white school of Syrie Maugham. But the last half of the 20th century was as exuberant as the 18th, starting with the unlikely fabrics and wallpapers of the 1950s that randomly spattered chianti bottles, red peppers and other exotica on white-backed cotton or created gloopy-looking fish on transparent plastic for the bathroom.

As well as the generally monochrome Timney and Fowler prints, which went from bed hangings and cushions onto T-shirts and silk jackets, Roger Saul at Mulberry went polychrome with nautical flags and heraldic devices, while outside influences were the ebullient wax-resist fabrics made for South-east Asia and Africa. Those made for the East are less extreme and generally based on indigo and white or, possibly, a third colour, while the African textiles praise their leaders to the skies with heroic portraits. There are also leaping dolphins, birds which turn into fish, be-finned American gas-guzzlers, buses and electric fans.

Despite their pictorial patterns, these fabrics are not hard to use. Since many patterns date back to the 17th and 18th centuries, they are excellent in rooms of those periods, as curtains, hangings, bed hangings and throws. Since they are all cotton, they work both in town and country, villa and cottage. Some illustrations are extremely sophisticated, others are naive. You can put together curtains of different toile patterns if you stick roughly to the same period and limit your colours to, say, indigo and rose madder, or the charming tobacco with cobalt. The Java and African fabrics should be held by a common and predominant shade, usually indigo or a strong brown. Around this can swirl as many yellows and reds as you wish. But keep Java away from Africa.

Chintz, too, mixes well if kept in period. The first patterns were basically Indian until Europe started to tinker with them. In southern France the Provençal pattern developed, while in Britain chintz evolved into classic florals. In the 18th century the craze for chinoiserie produced exotic mandarins and temples in lumpy landscapes and Chinese motifs which are direct descendants of the hand-painted Chinese wallpaper still found in grand houses.

THE COMPONENTS

Cushions, curtains and covers of all kinds represent the keynote elements of your chosen style, and offer great opportunities for decorative flair and innovation.

window dressings

Scandinavian style, classical and pared to essentials, has recently redefined the use of sheer fabrics for windows. It was the interest in paintings of Scandinavian interiors of the 18th and early 19th centuries – where plain casement and sash windows are almost always simply curtained with acres of white and off-white voile – that sparked the return of simple hangings. Since then we have become more relaxed and rediscovered an interest in the Orient. Following fashion trends, curtains now have Eastern fabrics as borders, cut-outs or panels.

Some time in the 1980s – at roughly the same moment as the whole world discovered that there was more to interiors than matching the background of the curtains with the beige carpet –the whole world went mad for curtains. Where once a few metres of floral chintz had been adequate, it seemed at this period as though we were trying to double the profits of the fabric companies. The chosen textiles had to be not only sumptuous and expensive but also ruched, swathed and folded as if there were no tomorrow – and they oozed over the floor like molten lava.

The excuse for all this showiness was that we were copying the authentic fashions of the 17th, 18th and 19th centuries, reflecting a mood that the last gasps of the 20th century should be as unrestrained and extravagant as other *fin de siècle* periods. This theory did not wholly wash, however, because the style in question was derived from palaces or, at the very least, from grand Georgian and Victorian piles. We were trying to create the same effect in modest terraced houses. Frankly, it was not a good moment in the annals of taste.

Reaction set in, and the 1990s saw curtains that were lean and slim and intended to cover our windows and our decency rather than make a statement about our wealth. Early in that period a Swedish writer, tackling one of those charming but spartan Scandinavian houses, described its curtains as 'like Strindberg'. I knew exactly what she meant.

ABOVE RIGHT AND OPPOSITE PAGE Simple fabrics can be given eccentric treatments. Here a hessian weave is shown to full advantage – the light from the window emphasizes its weave and fringed hems. From a foot below the window top, the curtain drops from wire clipped into metal eyes; more wire attaches it to the floor.

RIGHT Fashionable clothes have recently been given borders made from shiny, oriental floral fabrics. There is no reason why the same technique should not be used to strengthen and adorn the edges of curtains and blinds. You will find that small fabric finds can go a long way when used like this.

BELOW In this unusual treatment for a curtain top, heavy plain silk has been stiffened and given strong metal eyelets. The eyelets have been designed to run smoothly along a thick metal rod.

curtains
Today's curtains eschew obvious extravagance. While the fabrics may be truly grand – antique 17th-century velvets, genuine old toiles, bleached and crumbling with age, French handwoven linens – they do not flounce like *grandes horizontales* on Parisian sofas. Their width is generous enough to avoid that stretched look of economy that students can't avoid, but there is nothing extra. Just enough of the hem lies on the floor to stop howling draughts blowing under the bottom of the curtains, and the lining and interlining are enough to provide warmth without excessive bulk.

Fabrics have calmed down as well. Where, ten years ago, there were gaudy striped silks lined with gaudy plains and braided with yet further complementary fabrics – not to mention rosettes, tassels, hanging silk ribbons and the like – we now prefer our curtains to make less obvious statements.

In my opinion, soft furnishings should never be allowed to become the main focus of a room. They represent the elements of the style you have chosen, but they should be subordinate to the pictures and the furniture. If you believe that you can ill afford to buy good (inexpensive) pictures and would prefer to spend money on grand curtains, think again. Good pictures are quite likely to be a cheaper option, and a better investment, and to provide more lasting pleasure.

However, the curtain fabric and the way the curtains are styled do emphasize the effect you are trying to achieve. Curtains represent the biggest area of fabric you are likely to have in a room, so a cotton gingham in a primary colour will immediately say country style; a French toile will hint at the 18th century; and a porridge-mix wool will tell everyone you are out of date, that you have not changed your curtains since the 1970s – or that you are daringly retro. Whatever you do, avoid flounces, and make your curtains rather modest and unassuming.

In a decade's time, the mood may have swung back to extravagance, so whenever you renew your curtains have a good look at what the decorators are doing and what swatches the best manufacturers are producing. If you are lucky enough to have limitless storage space, hang onto your discards. What goes around comes around, and if you keep old textiles long enough they'll sell for a premium. I've never been able to throw

LEFT In reaction to the excesses of the 1980s, today's curtains do not ooze all over the floor – but these opalescent silk curtains have been given a heavy, exceptionally deep hem to drop them to floor level.

OPPOSITE PAGE, ABOVE RIGHT Grandeur doesn't come only with grand fabrics. This scheme uses a neutral check for the curtains, with complementary fabrics for the cushions and upholstery. Yet it has an air of refined luxury.

OPPOSITE PAGE, BELOW RIGHT A monochrome striped taffeta is used for these complex curtains (which actually have chintz inner curtains). Instead of pleats, they hang in bunches, while the sides are kept plain and straight.

LEFT A highly complex French striped fabric has been used for the walls, curtains and cushions of this grand room. It works because the colours are subtle and soft and because nothing else fights with the pattern.

away a good design. At the moment my bottom drawers are full of Arts and Crafts designs – which are currently out of fashion – along with linen union chintz.

Fortunately, we seem to have got over the collective obsession with giving our curtains linings, interlinings, underlinings and superlinings. While it may be important for curtains, when drawn, to be heavy enough to ensure that they do not billow out of the window, this can be achieved with lead weights carefully sited in the hems.

Personally, I like my curtains to have a touch of translucence so that you can see their weave at night and at dawn in the first sun's rays. All that is needed to achieve this is a single cotton lining, preferably in a strong complementary colour rather than dreary old beige.

ABOVE Some old patchwork quilts were made from worn-out men's shirts and this red and white version could be one of these. If you pick a single colour for quilt and curtains, it is possible to work with dozens of different types of check.

RIGHT The overscaled patterns used in the double curtains of this country room are far more interesting than a simple stripe and gingham would be.

OPPOSITE PAGE, LEFT A fine natural cotton with a heavy ruched top covers the window, while the heavier cotton curtain to the right has been used to divide off a small bathroom. The stool has a seat made from woven thrift-shop ties.

OPPOSITE PAGE, ABOVE RIGHT Tiny metal grippers along a metal rod hold linen hand towels used as plain half-curtains above wooden shutters. Such towels can be found in flea markets throughout Europe.

OPPOSITE PAGE, BELOW RIGHT In a flash of ingenuity, the owner has used striped and textured throws instead of curtains. The fringes at the ends are tied and hung on a metal rod.

pelmets Gone are the days when it was enough to get a strip of curtain fabric, ruch it up and call it a pelmet. There are better ways to remove your curtain track (the main purpose of a pelmet), such as fabric loops or ties and hooks, so you may not need a pelmet at all. However, if you decide that you do want one, you should have it made professionally. Even the simplest pelmet is hard to achieve without telltale unprofessional creases or tucks or faulty pattern matches. If you can't do it well, don't do it at all.

Alternatives to pelmets include small brass or iron grips, looped to run along brass curtain poles, that hold up the curtain fabric by pinching it at regular intervals. They originated in France and Italy but can now be found in all good curtain shops. The advantage is that you can hang anything in this way, from an antique dishcloth to a priceless Chinese silk, and it will become a curtain; the disadvantage is that, with rough treatment, the fabric will break free from the grips and slither to the floor.

Victorian curtain rings work on the same principle but are sewn onto the fabric, which stops the slithering but can damage a precious antique textile. Other systems of hanging fabrics, such as square tabard tops to the curtains

which act as runners on a track, or fancy tied ribbons over the pole were smart in the 1980s. If you are lucky enough to have a good decorator or curtain maker, consider a tailored pelmet – a straight screen for the track made in the same fabric as the curtain and stiffened from within. It can be perfectly straight or cut and bracketed in a way that harmonizes with the architecture of the room. It may also be quietly braided in a matching plain fabric or twisted cord.

How ornate you choose to be depends on the room. Bedrooms can absorb a few flounces. Dining rooms are often formal and a touch ornate, while living rooms should be carefully thought out because they are where you spend most of your time. Avoid any fanciness in a bathroom or a kitchen because flounces catch the grease and steam and look tired in no time. In hot countries, they encourage snakes and scorpions too.

OPPOSITE PAGE Although this pelmet draws its inspiration from the 18th century, it has a pared-down – yet grand – 21st-century feel. The tassels and ornamental pleats make sure the the treatment is noticed, but there is not a ruch or a swag in sight.

ABOVE LEFT One of the 18th century's charmingly flowered cotton fabrics is used both for curtains and for the simple boxed pelmet above.

LEFT Chinese celadon green with soft creams forms the basis of this calm sitting room. Blue and white checks of different scales have been added to achieve an extra lift.

blinds

Blinds are a modern solution to blocking out windows at night or shielding an interior from strong sunlight. They offer the advantage of revealing any interesting architectural detail in the window surround while maximizing the light that comes in through the panes. A well-designed blind leaves the window sill clear in a bathroom or gives a few centimetres of additional space to a small room.

Fashions in blinds can be extreme, and a style that has lost its clout soon looks naff. Consider, for instance, the dreadful fate of the Austrian ruched blind. Where, 20 years ago, it was smart, now it is regarded as worse than any other window hanging – even the Venetian blind, which suffered the same demise a decade before. Simpler blinds are less vulnerable to the whims of fashion. The pleated Roman blinds – which pull up into a neat rectangle of fabric and let down into a similarly unadorned length of fabric – are still very acceptable,

especially if you pick a suitable style of fabric. This might be a good-looking, strong-coloured plain (pale colours quickly show dirt in the folds) or a pictorial that can stand daily exposure without becoming boring. Indeed, if you are particularly fond of a pictorial fabric, a blind is the best way to show it off.

A roller blind offers an equally good means of maximizing the light from a window. The rolled-up blind does not cover the panes at all, and when the blind is pulled down the glass is concealed by a good-looking

ABOVE What could be simpler than this neutral Roman blind made of calico? Yet not only does it cover the glass with the minimum of fuss but it allows the architecture to speak for itself. Such blinds are excellent where space is limited.
LEFT Dramatic architecture demands dramatic treatment. Roller blinds don't have to start at the top of a large window and end at the bottom – as this hard-edged modern room demonstrates. Plain white blinds are the least assertive of window coverings. They are perfect for all minimalist interiors, for disguising ugly views and, in bedrooms, offering privacy.

THIS PAGE Office? Living room? Loft? The plain white blinds in this simple modern room allow its purpose to be adapted at will from cool interior to room with a view.

OPPOSITE PAGE Blinds do not have to be made of opaque fabrics. A fine white voile is left unlined in this Roman version, allowing a diffused light into the room.

BELOW Fine fabrics such as cotton voiles can be made more or less opaque by layering. Here there is both a blind and curtains of the same fabric.

LEFT Roman blinds made out of voile, as in this example, produce interesting shades and tones as the fabric is doubled and redoubled.

fabric – or even by a version of a scene or a painting that glows with the moonlight behind it. The problem with roller blinds is that the mechanisms can be unreliable and need a professional to make them well.

How many times has a roller refused to roll or gone up wonky? How often have you found that it won't quite complete its journey in either direction? Or, worse, that it snaps out of your hand and biffs you? Personally, I'd leave the bad-tempered things alone until someone invents a better mechanism (which may be centuries because inventors are all so busy mucking about with computers).

I'm not sure whether those half or full lengths of stretched cloth found in Italian homes and French bistros count as curtains or as blinds, but – because they are not intended to draw and have no pleats – I shall treat them as blinds. If you can find the ideal white linen or cotton embroidered fabric with cut-out patterns, these blinds are charming in bathrooms and kitchens and, if your room is overlooked, make an excellent alternative to the ubiquitous net curtains. They can also be washed with ease.

However, they don't look right in Britain or America in large windows and should be kept for smaller windows and glass doors only – otherwise your house will resemble a French railway cottage. An alternative is go back to the screens of the 18th and 19th centuries. These were made of oiled silk and often in colours as garish as the colour of an oilcloth. They do look very strange – and bring a weird light into a room – but they are authentic.

If you need a blind at the window instead of a curtain, it is best to keep it simple. A plain white roller or Roman version will shield you very well and draw no attention to itself. If, then, you can add a pair of beautiful curtains that never need to be drawn (saving money on the fabric) you will have the best of both worlds.

sheers

Sheers were deeply unfashionable for decades because – I suppose – they were seen as no different from the net curtains that covered every window in suburbia, reducing light indoors while discouraging prying eyes. The theory was that, if you didn't live in the inner city or suburbia, if your neighbours never got near enough to pry, then you didn't need net curtains. No doubt, in the John Betjeman view of the world, nets were crass.

BELOW LEFT Fine cotton curtains do not keep out the light but provide privacy in a country bedroom. The inner half-curtain remains drawn, while the floral outer one is casually tied.
BELOW White sheer fabrics can be used both to blot out an unwanted view and to enhance the bits worth seeing. Even in daylight, the effect will be light and cool.
OPPOSITE PAGE, CENTRE LEFT Translucent fabrics allow diffused light into rooms during the day, and when the sun shines they pick up architectural patterns from the windows behind.

The Scandinavians have taught us to appreciate sheer fabrics that can block views from outside of our lighted rooms at night while allowing plenty of sunshine to flood in during the day. On warm and sunny days, open windows also allow the fabric to billow in the sun, giving a fine, fresh feeling. With their limited hours of daylight, northern Europeans know all about making the most of the sun when it does appear.

Conversely, we have also been influenced in our love of voiles, nets and muslins by the tropical and Mediterranean countries. A fashion for hanging mosquito nets over our insect-free beds led us to realize how charming unadorned, light-textured nets could be as bed hangings. The brilliantly dyed muslins of India have also appeared as bed hangings, with colour over

RIGHT Self-patterned sheer curtains are good for large windows and help to accentuate the little balcony. The deep ruffle at the top has the effect of a pelmet.

BOTTOM LEFT Raid granny's linen cupboard for such exquisite needlework as this drawn threadwork half-curtain. A red crochet trimming is an extra benefit.

BOTTOM RIGHT It seems obvious to convert pretty linen tea towels into curtains for small windows. They have their own coloured edging and wash like a dream.

RIGHT Curtains can be used like screens to make temporary divisions in large or awkward rooms. This beautiful mixture of velvet and organza also hints at what is beyond.
BELOW Translucent voile is mounted as a screen to divide two rooms. It's an excellent way to borrow light from one to another.

colour creating rich mixtures of tone and shade. This is the hippy look, which first arrived on bead-strung dresses and kaftans in the 1970s and is certainly due for a revival.

From the Mediterranean we learned to love the simplicity of thin white cotton, hung without ruches or bunching at cottage windows. Teamed with casements painted in the evocative colours of Greece and Italy – an Ionian blue, a Tuscan terracotta – white fabric brings a country charm while emphasizing the colours of the paintwork around it. Thin white cotton with age-old patterns cut in the fabric has been used as an alternative to net curtains in France and Italy. Strung on a brass rail, either at the top or halfway down the window, it is a far prettier

solution for those whose houses are next to a busy road. Take a tip from the Italians and use it to hide the contents of glazed cupboards too. In a kitchen, living room or bathroom, this simple cotton will hide multicoloured clutter with charm – and it can be washed as easily as bed linen.

Sheer fabrics, by which I mean cotton in all its forms, are relatively cheap, drape well and are lightweight, even if used in bulk. (Don't even think about synthetics, which somehow look both unpleasantly shiny and dirty within minutes.) Swedish-style voile curtains, for example, should consist of masses of fabric so that, pulled together with curtain tape, they provide a good screen against the world. Voile hangings on beds can be simply draped over the posts, while doors too can be curtained with sheers that, on hot days, allow in cool breezes while providing privacy.

If your house is in a place where the summer and winter temperatures vary between extremes (as in many areas of the Mediterranean), it is worth thinking about using sheer hangings for summer only. As autumn arrives, these can be changed for heavier wools, which provide a comforting warmth and won't billow in the breeze.

THIS PAGE This room is furnished entirely in neutral shades. The interest lies in the textures, from the fur rug and faux fur cover of the sofa to the softly uplit voile curtains.

loose covers and upholstery

Loose covers got a bad name in the 1930s and after, when most of them seem to have been made in exuberantly flowered chintz designed by a begonia specialist. The typical cover was made up to resemble a large fat lady with a penchant for frills around her ankles. The early 20th-century covered sofa was a monster. By contrast, today's loose cover is almost indistinguishable from the upholstery beneath.

The modern loose cover is a neatly tailored job whose style is far less – well – loose than that which characterized its 20th-century predecessors. Indeed, it may be difficult to tell the loose cover apart from the upholstery beneath it. Frills have become anathema. Either the sofa's feet are allowed to peep out under it or the frill has given way to a neat edging – and blowsy chintzes have been consigned to the fashion dustbin.

Today's fabrics for loose covers are generally plain and neutral – which has the effect of reducing the apparent bulk of a sofa or chair – or they may be found in geometrics such as checks and stripes. If chintz is used, the design is likely to be one of the stricter versions, with flowers arranged in stripes or in such as way as to

LEFT This highly styled drawing room is characterized by neutral colours, but walls, curtains and cushions are overprinted, seamed, embroidered, woven and appliquéd to achieve a rich combination of textures.
BELOW LEFT When a room is full of interesting objects, the furniture can take second place, but this quietly upholstered sofa contributes to the modernist feel with its strong lines. The throw is equally quietly folded.
OPPOSITE PAGE, LEFT Leopard – even faux leopard – is in natural camouflage shades and, while the pattern in the room can be emphatic, it fits in well with old wooden flooring.
OPPOSITE PAGE, RIGHT Mattress ticking is tightly woven to keep the feathers from escaping and it therefore makes an excellent upholstery fabric for chairs and sofas. Contrast piping on this Knole sofa defines the soft stripe.

create a firm, overall pattern. Sensibly, a great deal of contemporary furniture is sold separately from its final upholstery. You can buy it with a plain cream cambric cover, ready for the added loose cover that suits your room (and protects the furniture against accidental spillages and potential damage by the children or the dog). Alternatively, you can order the upholstery fabric from the manufacturer.

If I had the opportunity, I would always take the cambric and search elsewhere for a fabric that will give the furniture a stamp of individuality. After all, who wants visitors to recognize the same fabric that has appeared on hundreds of other sofas and chairs?

Added to that, I would be inclined to invest in two contrasting sets of loose covers, one that is suitable for summer and one for winter. This offers the advantage that, while one set is being washed and rested, the other can be used on the furniture, giving a totally new, seasonal look to your room. Mind you, I haven't actually done this yet – but it's on my wish list.

sofas

Sofas are for lounging on. Even such belles as Madame Recamier, in Jacques-Louis David's painting, and Pauline Borghese, sculpted nude by Canova, are convincingly relaxed as they lie on their day beds – and we should be too. Of course, we would not be happy slopping about with the kids and the dog if we knew that beneath our bums and feet lay a fabric that cost a hundred pounds a metre, not to mention the hundreds more needed to re-upholster it. Modern sofa makers have come up with the idea of selling their pieces covered simply in calico, awaiting a proper cover – or, if the sofa is going to fulfil its perfect role, a loose cover.

I think that all sofas (unless upholstered in forgiving leather) need loose covers. You can take off a loose cover for a party, to reveal the glory of the fabric underneath, but if you don't have a cover you'll never enjoy your sofa.

Many loose covers also have piping in complementary colours or, when the main fabric is patterned, one shade is picked out. Piping gives definition to the shape of the sofa – use it if you want the piece to stand out in a

BELOW LEFT A single spot of colour in a neutral room is provided by a sofa covered in a lush raspberry. The neutral theme of the rest of the design is picked up in the two cushions, which have bands of hessian as a detail.
BELOW The strong lines of an upright sofa predominate in this scheme,

though the upholstered base and bolsters are made from an exceptionally pretty cotton stitched with flowers.
OPPOSITE PAGE Special saleroom buys of interesting old or expensive fabrics can be appliquéd onto plain cushions to give colour and texture without incurring too much expense.

FAR LEFT Everything in this living room has been chosen to focus attention on the black and white photograph on the end wall. If you have an assertive picture, it is a sensible strategy to theme a room around it.

LEFT When a room already possesses a decorative feature such as this arched window with its pure blue stained-glass detail, why fuss it up? The owner has left all the soft furnishings in shades of cream and white with a single touch of blue on a cushion.

room; if you want it to be less obtrusive, look for a darkish neutral that picks up colours in the carpet, walls or curtains. Try to hide its ugly back with a prettier piece of furniture – a sofa table, for example, or a painted chest or screen.

An alternative to the loose cover is a throw. One advantage of a throw is that, because it does not have to be tailored to fit, it is likely to be cheaper than a loose cover. A selection of throws allows you to change the mood of a room – pinstriped flannel for winter, for instance, changing to beaded African indigo for summer. Or you can change the throw according to circumstances. The dog may have its own washable blanket, but the day friends come round you can drape the sofa in cashmere or a paisley shawl.

Choose the throw with the whole room in mind: the colours should complement the rest of the decor and the pattern should make it clear whether you want to emphasize the fabric or leave it unobtrusive. Neither loose

cover nor throw needs to be washable (though in a large family it helps), but it does need to be dry-cleanable. It should be made of a welcoming fabric; neither horsehair nor shiny silk is conducive to lounging, while corduroy, tweed, flannel and linen are. And – while you may not want to encourage nudes to relax on the sofa in imitation of Manet's odalisque – the fabric you choose should at least be generous to naked arms, legs and feet.

ABOVE Deep-buttoned sofas can be made less formal with plain upholstery and plenty of added checks and stripes.
OPPOSITE PAGE A raw-silk seat, deep-buttoned, adds comfort to a plain dark sofa, also in raw silk. The cushions are of tie-dyed cotton.

armchairs

Armchairs are a bit easier to deal with than sofas because they are smaller and less obtrusive in a room, but the same principles apply: easy chairs should be easy. As with sofas, I would use loose covers to keep worry at bay, except in the case of those deep club chairs made of leather so sat-upon that it is as soft as velvet. The tailored cushions, often of brown velvet, should be covered, however – perhaps in a similar, but washable, corduroy.

Avoid the three-piece suite. Have three pieces if you like – but don't have them en suite. While the armchairs and sofa may all be made to the same shape and pattern, make sure that you cover the three differently. For example, the chairs might be in the multicoloured stripe that is taking over from ticking – beige, stone, white, cobalt blue and terracotta in varying widths – while the sofa is covered with a plain fabric in one of these shades or in a simpler version of the stripe. Add complementary plain and patterned throws for extra comfort and informality. This will give the room a less formal and bulky look.

A pair of armchairs, minus sofa, can be treated in the same way or, especially if they are not the same shape, covered with the same fabric so that they don't look like random buys. You can also upholster armchairs in similar fabrics even if they are not in the same room. You may need to bring extra chairs into the main living room when more people are at home and it helps if they complement the chairs that are already there.

ABOVE The price of new armchairs, not to mention their style, puts them out of the contest. Old 1930s pieces can be found cheaply, restored and upholstered in your own fabric for far less.

ABOVE Modern curing techniques, which have made suede washable, mean that covering a chair with the palest hides need not be totally impractical.
RIGHT In this hard-edged scheme, the shiny texture of the glass-topped trestle table has been emphasized by the taut, shiny leather that covers the armchair.

ABOVE Buy old chairs with comfortable lines and get a new cover to fit your scheme. If the fabric is pale, make sure that it is washable and loose.

THIS PAGE A modern chair with an unusual swivel base has been covered in an unlikely deep-buttoned patterned cotton – but it works. One way to draw attention to interesting pieces of furniture is to cover them in fabrics which, at first, seem unsuitable.

LEFT AND FAR LEFT Traditional French tickings tended to match each other because they were produced from natural and bleached linen in indigo or madder stripes. This style of ticking is being recreated today, and is ideal for introducing colour and freshness to the seating area of an informal dining room. A more interesting effect is achieved by picking variations on a theme rather than going for an exact match. Details such as the cross-gartered legs of the chairs and the bold, complementary cotton cloth on the table simply add extra elements of fun to the lively scheme.

dining chairs

Upright wooden chairs that may be used anywhere in the home from the kitchen to the office can be great fun to upholster. This is partly because they demand such a small quantity of fabric that you can afford to choose something pretty expensive. Also, it is much harder than with armchairs to make a mistake. I recently covered the drop-in seat of a Regency chair with fake leopard skin and it looked terrific. Equally successful was a set of eight 18th-century chairs I once saw in a dining room each covered with a different exotic fake fur, including cheetah, leopard, tiger, zebra and giraffe. Or you could try bits of antique paisley shawl (one too far gone for restoration) or a scrap of ancient toile de Jouy.

The wooden seats of country chairs are always more comfortable with cushions, which can be dressed up with striped silk or dressed down with old denim. Avoid obtrusive bows and clever bits. A cushion should ideally be a simple pad in a wonderful fabric that allows the chair to show its own character.

Of course, you may not have decent chairs – in which case, they can be encased in loose covers in the way they were in the 18th century when a country house was shut down for the season. Find a set of the cheapest chairs you can afford (making sure that their underlying shape is simple) and cover them with a good plain stripe or check, possibly piped in a contrasting fabric. I myself would never make these chair covers into little girls' frocks with gigantic bows on their rears, but I do see that dining rooms need, occasionally, to show off. If you like the idea of covering cheap chairs, it is worth doing the sums in advance. Add the cost of the fabric (and its making up) to the cost of the chairs – you may find that it is cheaper in the long run to buy more expensive chairs at the start.

OPPOSITE PAGE, FAR RIGHT ABOVE AND BELOW In the case of dining chairs, the back is just as important as the front. Choose the fabric with care and make sure the detailing – piping, pattern and so on – is exactly tailored. The chair backs are what people see most often.
OPPOSITE PAGE, BOTTOM LEFT The strict form of the modernist chair, upholstered in a severe grey fabric, has been relaxed by a generous cushion in a lighter and friendlier pastel shade.
OPPOSITE PAGE, BOTTOM CENTRE Dining chairs can be both colourful and funny. This seat is made from interwoven silk ties. What makes it work is the strong blue and white element.

RIGHT AND BELOW A simple French chair, painted a typically soft grey, has been upholstered in a plain red and white gingham. But what makes this upholstery different is the way the double piping has been used diagonally to frame the chair back and seat. Genius is in the detail.

cushions

Cushions as we know them are essentially a modern invention, as is the easy armchair. Lounging, except on couches (Roman orgy scenes) or day beds (Elizabeth Barrett repining), was not part of ordinary life until the 20th century. By the time we entered the 21st century, we had got our cushions down to a fine art.

Cushions are the perfect accessory in a room. Like a chap's colourful tie worn with a grey suit, they are not strictly necessary and fulfil no particular function, but they are an expression of personality. People may, of course, disagree that they have no function – but how often do you see them expressly discarded from a chair or sofa? As for that fashionable heap of cushions on a double bed – they all have to be removed before you can get in and snuggle down.

Cushions represent movable areas of colour – contrasting, complementary and changing with the seasons, as well as giving an impression of luxury. While they are one of the cheapest and easiest-to-make forms of upholstery – even I could sew up a cushion cover, if pressed – great mountains of well-chosen cushions really do give the impression that a room is cherished.

There are rules about how to get the best from cushions. Here are a few don'ts. Never, ever, fill them with anything but feathers. Kapok, cut-up bits of plastic foam or solid chunks of foam always look lumpy and are uncomfortable to recline against. Never, ever, array your cushions on their corners and, especially, don't colour-theme them in strict order. One multimillionaire does exactly this: each sofa has a row of diamond-ended cushions in

RIGHT Fabrics are used here to soften severe lines: cushions are appliquéd and overstitched; floor cushions have extra mats.
BELOW A coffee-brown day bed is upholstered in suede, whose texture contrasts with that of the calico cushions.

BELOW LEFT Earth-tone neutral cushions are given a lift by being covered in a soft muslin with knotted ties at the side.
BELOW These cushions of alligator and ostrich come from farms where the animals are bred for their meat. But, for interior designers, their skins are far more tasty.

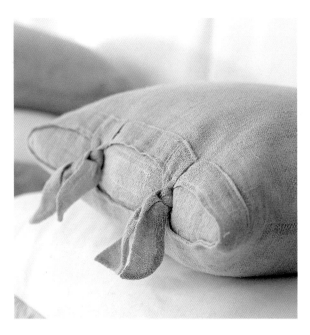

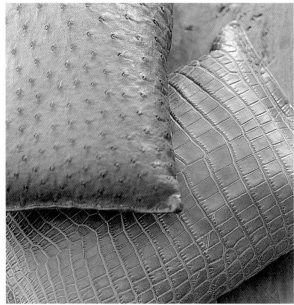

red/green, red/green rows – it looks as though no one has ever sat on the sofas. Don't make cushions all the same size; don't make them too small (or too large), for neither will be comfortable against your back. Don't overdo the frills, tassels, braiding and other furbelows. I prefer a few squares and rectangles, neatly piped with unfussy matching or complementary fabric, and backed with the same fabric or matching – cheaper – lining, but I do see that this might be too austere for some rooms.

Where you can enjoy yourself is in choosing the fabrics. For a start, cushion fabrics can be quite expensive because you will need less than a square metre if you cover one side of the cushion only. You can find scraps in sales, samples and bin-end boxes, along with scraps of antique tapestries, or ancient paisley shawls too worn to be usable whole. The same goes for Victorian quilts that have seen better days or scraps of damask from some grand old curtains. Even if these are frayed, bleached by the sun or patched in places, it does not matter.

Little scraps of embroidery can be appliquéd onto a cushion, or you can go for the full needlepoint treatment. You may be tempted to embark on cushions in the grand manner: the Duchess of Windsor had images of her pugs embroidered onto piles of cushions, while

ABOVE Cushions are becoming increasingly detailed. Here, a dark brown velvet cushion has been given a flap and oriental button detail while, in front, Eastern raw silks have a tiny knotted fastening.

RIGHT Cushions as stars: each one of these is made of assertive colours and fabrics – especially the multicoloured cover of woven velvet ribbons, which could be made by the most unhandy of us.

OPPOSITE PAGE

TOP ROW LEFT Voile can be sewn on above a different colour, as in these cushions, which have a gold voile top over purple cotton fabric beneath.

TOP ROW CENTRE Stripes of bright silk fabric give a glow to a sombre wooden sofa.

TOP ROW RIGHT Detailed overstitched flowers are carefully shaded to bring the colours together.

BOTTOM ROW LEFT Indian or North African markets – or similar stores in ethnically mixed towns and cities – can provide treasures such as woven saris, which make superb cushion covers.

BOTTOM ROW RIGHT A red felt backing has been used on a sofa to accentuate the strong stripes of silk and taffeta cushions, formally positioned.

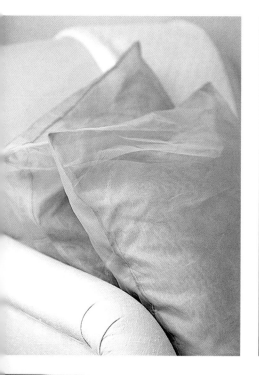

RIGHT Old sheets are simply thrown over easy chairs to make plain, washable covers, while plain voiles are knotted at the windows. Otherwise, brilliant quilts and florals are strewn about the room.
BELOW A detail from the room shows how strong colours – in this case an old patchwork quilt and antique flowery cushion – can be made to work together.

that clever collector Lord McAlpine had flowers and urns on cushions in his Hampshire house. Nor do you need to be too skilled or patient with a needle – embroidered cushions are quite undemanding. You can even invent your own designs which, if complicated, can be translated onto a tapestry by a professional.

When you are piling up these treasures, make sure that the heap is not too busy with different fabrics, shapes, textures and colours. If you restrict yourself to one type of fabric – early greeny-blue tapestry bits, for instance – you can indulge in quite a few different shapes and sizes, and

even add some cushions in a similar but plain wool cloth. If you are enthusiastic about pictorial cottons such as toile de Jouy or Timney and Fowler's reworked classics, keep to one colour mixture; if you want a whole collection of cushions in unpatterned peacock- and midnight-blue fabrics, you can combine flannel with damask and silk and it will still look good. But coordinate the whole with the chairs and sofas on which the cushions are piled and with the room in general.

The modern attitude is to regard cushions as wonderfully luxurious neutrals. The most fashionable interiors have cushions piled in tower blocks, coloured in a variety of whites – oatmeal, bone and stone. They are subdued and subtle in their impact but created from soft wool knitted in the patterns of fishermen's sweaters or in heavy teased cashmere.

Our preoccupation with natural themes has led to cushions delicately buttoned in horn or bone or adorned with pieces of spotted seashell or wooden toggles. They have a smart, tailored look and are equally at home in a modern Manhattan loft and a seaside boathouse. Glossy magazines show anonymous figures lounging on these piles, hugging them to their chests or perching on piles on the floor – and this is how they are supposed to be treated. This is the cushion at its most comfortable yet.

Cushions in the bedroom are also intended to be sybaritic. They can be rather more frilled and fancy than those in the living room – lace backed with a contrasting colour, for example, or white linen embroidered in Chinese white. Pile them high on every bed, with big square continental pillows at the bottom and smaller, prettier pieces on top. Bedroom pillows should suggest the bed linen beneath and seem to be washable and fresh.

If the bed is a four-poster with hangings, or the room is feminine and floral, add some of the floral fabric in among the plainer, whiter versions. Cushions on bedroom chairs, however, should revert to the stouter, living-room style – perhaps in fabric versions of the room's wallpaper or a cloth which complements the curtains. As with any decoration, don't have everything matching – it always looks forced.

There are a few other areas that benefit from cushions. Wide windows, especially those with fine views, are perfect for window seats, as are the cane chairs often found in garden rooms. The cushions for chairs sited

LEFT Generously sized and overstuffed chairs should be given the country house treatment with softly coloured chintz covers. Try to find a matching fabric for the cushions. Snap up old chairs with well-washed loose covers where you can (house sales are good) for they have a softness that contemporary reproductions rarely achieve. But don't despair if you have to buy a new loose cover – repeated washing soon achieves the desired effect. **ABOVE** Texture is given particular prominence in this all-white scheme, which shows triumph in the detail.

among plants look excellent in green and white leafy fabric or in green and white stripes and gingham. The brilliant green makes the plants look more abundant and healthier.

Cushions are great outdoors, too. A grand Italian hotel has square iron chairs on each of its verandahs and their loose cushions, upholstered in a soft, creamy wool, are moved each night (and when rain is threatened) onto iron stands made specially to accommodate them. Martha Stewart keeps the cushions for her outdoor chairs in a giant lightweight basket by the garden door so they

BELOW AND RIGHT These cushions are covered in a beautiful – and, no doubt, expensive – fabric in subtle strips of tobacco, ecru and charcoal. It makes practical sense to spend money on fabrics for cushions because, when only small quantities are needed, the effect is out of all proportion to the cost.

ABOVE Buttons, shells and personal mementoes can easily be sewn onto cushions for an individual look. Use thread matching the cushion rather than the objects.
RIGHT Covers appliquéd with circles and chequerboards can be machined together from linens and silks found in sales.
BELOW These cushions are covered in fabric from the same maker but in different neutrals. One shade is picked up in the soft wool throw, another in the carpet.

can be brought in and out depending on the weather. Another clever idea for cushions is to alternate them with the seasons, as Tricia Guild does in her Tuscan house. Summer, especially in the Mediterranean, has the kind of light that is ideal for strong colours and fine cotton weaves; winter is better suited to cushions made from chunky wool blankets like those in subtly coloured checks and stripes from the Welsh firm of Melin Tregwynt. Shades of toning grey and white, or dark purple with deep terracotta, make a room cosy, especially when the gales are howling outside.

Cushions add the finishing touches to a living room or bedroom and, by changing them regularly, you will define and update the whole.

FAR RIGHT ABOVE AND BELOW
The designer of this room has used soft shades of beige, pink and white to create a sophisticated and restful space. Even the books in the shelves are in keeping. Subtle neutral fabrics make adaptable cushion covers which can be moved from room to room. It is a good idea to use plain rather than contrast piping and to keep things simple.

bed furnishings

People should be prejudiced about their beds and the linen they use. It's the most personal form of decor in the house. I know a troupe of actors who refuse to stay on tour at any hotel or B&B that has nylon sheets or blankets – otherwise they cannot sleep well enough to give a good performance the next day. I've stayed in a self-catering castle where the cheapest nylon blankets – in purple, for heaven's sake – were considered adequate for the guests. Such dreadful offerings are never forgotten.

LEFT A bedroom of soft beige and white artfully uses cotton hangings to give scale to the bed. The shades are picked up in six small rugs and in the piled pillows and cushions.

My own prejudice is to have everything white. Years of sleeping in dark brown sheets or covered in psychedelic duvets covers – survivors from the 1970s – have taken their toll. If I were really rich, I would define this even further and use only pure linen, but that extravagance is beyond me, apart from a pair of wonderful linen pillowcases I bought in an antique shop in Suffolk.

It's hard to be dogmatic about bed linen except to say that comfort should be the first object. If black satin is comfortable, then have it; if you prefer a duvet stuffed with the finest silk or the softest goose down, have that too. Next, bed linen should always be fresh, so find a fabric that is easy to clean or, better still, to wash. That's why I prefer all white – no complications in the washing machine – and I'm not keen on any but the simplest pattern. Curves and swirls and surrealist flowers are not relaxing, and I wonder how any child can sleep under bed linen printed with dinosaurs or space stations. Stripes, however, are fine, and I'm occasionally tempted by fine sheets edged in a soft but contrasting shade. Liberty's bed linen once used deliciously crackling organza in shades such as charcoal and prune over softer, more comfortable sheets of paler fabrics.

Linen, however, seems to be getting cheaper and more readily available, and much of it comes from Russia. If you are rich enough, it makes sense to buy in bulk and get special rates for your buy (try an Irish wholesale firm, for instance) or to purchase one pair of sheets a year, which means that they won't all wear out at once. Failing that, good-quality cotton is extremely comfortable and easy to wash. I am always on the lookout in junk shops for hardly used bedlinen. It's surprisingly cheap compared to new versions and, if you're happy sleeping in much-used hotel sheets, why get worried about private ones?

Antique and second-hand sheets are always white or off-white. It wasn't until the 1960s that the coloured and patterned sheet – that aberration of nature – made its appearance.

bed linen
The colour you choose for your bed linen may come in a variety of shades. White, for example, ranges from the sharpest white of ironed linen to the soft fuzzy creams of blankets and the blue notes of seersucker on the duvet. The same trick can be worked with a pastel colour, where it is also possible to add deeper tones of the primary colour for stitching and edging. So choose all the bed linen – pillowcases, sheets, blankets and duvet covers – to look good together.

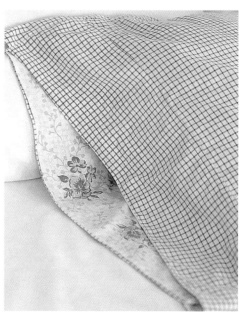

ABOVE Fresh white bedlinen is always beautiful. In this cool naturalistic setting, the sheer voile curtains and off-white panelling provide a haven from the outside glare.

ABOVE CENTRE Sumptuous cashmere cushions are set against linen pillows, while a cotton knit bedspread is offset by a muted paisley throw. White is an extremely good background for showing off textures, especially in the bedroom.

RIGHT A checked cotton gingham covers the walls of a charming bedroom. The soft greens are picked up by a bedcover strewn with embroidered flowers while the pillows have a more complex version of the pattern.

TOP This ingenious bed hanging has deep pockets sewn into it – which make useful receptacles for paperbacks, handkerchiefs and alarm clocks. More substantial storage space can be found under the bed, in the form of large wicker drawers on wheels.

ABOVE A monochrome blue and white floral in the 19th-century style is matched with a simple windowpane-check cotton. The charm of soft furnishings is usually to be found in the details.

RIGHT Square continental pillows are covered with crisp, embroidered and hemstitched linen (look out for them in antique shops). The damask-covered bedside table and tiny 19th-century all-over print on the coverlet are neat touches.

BELOW RIGHT Bright white cotton sheets and a waffle blanket in a creamier colour are given a lift by floral cushions casually placed.

If your bathroom is en suite, it is probably a good idea to coordinate bath towels, flannels, slippers and dressing gown with the bedroom decor because you will be using those items in both the bathroom and bedroom. Towels, bathmats and flannels really should be plain and, if you want to add luxury, buy nothing but the best-quality towelling you can afford.

Dressing gowns, slippers, and so on, can be a little more individual, but make sure that they complement the bedroom and bathroom. They probably will because, if a certain colour in clothes doesn't suit you, you probably won't want to use that colour anywhere else.

Like sheets and pillowcases, towels and bathroom fabrics should be scrupulously fresh, although only the very rich and very pernickety insist that sheets should be ironed every day and towels consigned to the laundry basket after every use.

Plain pale colours enhance the impression of freshness, while plain dark colours create exactly the opposite effect. Why would anyone choose black towels or black sheets if not to hide the dirt? This may not be a valid deduction, but it's the thought that counts.

Finally, use the power of scent to enhance the look you have decided on. Quite a few cosmetic firms – notably Jo Malone, Penhaligons and Crabtree and Evelyn – produce aerosols of scent to spray on bed linen. The notes of citrus, lime and spices not only emphasize the pleasures of newly ironed laundry but also help you to sleep.

bed hangings

The hangings on four-poster beds are more than purely decorative. Today, they keep out draughts and make us feel secure. In the 19th century they were an important instrument of privacy because, in houses with no corridors and servants constantly on the move, the bedroom was no more private than any other room – but the bed was.

Four posters have seen a remarkable revival. Hung with cleverly draped curtains and false fabric ceilings, they turn a bedroom from a mundane sleeping area into something special. Hangings come in a huge range of styles and fabrics, from rich silks, patterned on the outside and lined with plains or simple patterns, to tartans, voiles and even men's wool worsted, pin- or chalk-striped. Hangings around a bed should be heavy enough to protect against winter draughts and fine enough to admit cool breezes, so you may need to change them with the change of season. Heavy linen in shades such as rich cream, pale indigo or terracotta may work all year round or, as autumn approaches, you can simply add an outer hanging of kilim or tapestry over the summer voile.

Bed hangings are meant to be showy, so be exuberant and generous with the fabric you choose. Hold back the curtains with tassels or gilded tiebacks and consider scalloping the hangings that hide the superstructure of the bed, as the French did in the 18th century. If you don't have a four-poster, you can still have fun with a corona applied to the wall directly above the bed. Fabric can issue from this and fan out round the bed head.

TOP Simple cotton muslin is draped around this old bed in a Belgian apartment.

ABOVE White cotton hangings and bed linen insulate the sleeper from everything but the trees outside.

RIGHT Mosquito nets may not be essential in London or Paris but they are certainly decorative. Add a slew of luxurious pinks on the white bed and you get a room that is ultra-modern yet totally feminine.

OPPOSITE PAGE, ABOVE LEFT Hangings always make a bed more romantic but they can make night-time reading tricky. Lights inside the fabric cocoon are both practical and charming.

OPPOSITE PAGE, BELOW LEFT A four-poster can be invented by hanging curtains from a ceiling moulding.

OPPOSITE PAGE, RIGHT The bed is the centre of this European–oriental room with its domed top, white hangings and Indian posts.

bedcovers and quilts

Quilts are more than pure bed coverings; they have a historical significance. In both Europe and America, quilting parties, or bees, were a way for women to congregate and chat while still being hard at work. Quilts might be created by communal effort or made for a bride or to commemorate an important event. From the sewn patterns of the plain Durham quilts to the exuberance of the American log-cabin and flower quilts, they were important.

Quilts should be treated with respect. Beautiful 19th-century patchwork quilts are still available, and there are plenty of handbooks to help enthusiasts to make their own patchworks. If you decide to do so, seek out an original and avoid, at all costs, those jumbles of hexagons in old dress cottons. A good quilt must have a strong presence.

I recently visited an exhibition of Amish quilts from Indiana, which had been brought to Britain by the American Museum in Bath. The Amish enforced strict laws about the colour of their clothes, which seeped through into their quilts. As a consequence, their work is characterized by subtle and unexpected combinations of colour. One quilt in the show was a mixture of steel blue, aubergine, aquamarine and coral; another mixed black with pink; and in another subfusc black and olive were enlivened with touches of crimson. Find, if you can, a book on the work of the Amish – and imitate it.

You may not want to draw too much attention to the quilt, however, which invariably happens with an antique. Good-looking quilts can be made of midnight-blue silk or plain ticking sewn into patterns; or you can

ABOVE A bedroom of Shaker-like simplicity lets its hair down with a colourful and complex American quilt. The curvy pattern contrasts with the severe lines of the drawers in the wall. **LEFT** Stripes of textured silk have been oversewn onto a shiny raw silk bedcover. The piles of cushions are covered in similar shades of silk. **RIGHT** Shades of indigo mingle in a rural bedroom. A striped cotton bedspread is offset by the plain valance beneath it, while blinds and lampshades are trimmed in blue.

RIGHT This American-style bedroom uses antique patchwork quilts both on the bed and as the hanging behind it. The brilliant blues are matched by French ticking cushion covers, the floor mat and the voile half-curtains.

copy the Durham idea of sewing feather patterns, roundels and squares onto plain cotton, giving the effect of blind printing. This can be done with a sewing machine as well as by hand. Durham women also sewed onto broad stripes.

A common fault with quilts is that they slither onto the floor as you sleep. If the fabric of the back (hidden) side is slightly rough, this is less likely to happen – so, if the top of your quilt is to be made of silk satin, use a slub underneath. But always remember that quilts will have to be washed or dry-cleaned regularly and should, therefore, be made of fabrics that will respond in the same way as each other. Of course, you may intend your antique beauty to be for show alone. That's fine – but your guests won't know that their quilt is worth hundreds of pounds. If your guest rooms have museum-quality quilts, take them off before you invite visitors.

valances and headboards
There is only one reason for having a valance – and that is to hide all the gubbins that go with the base of a bed. Their effect should be subtle and unobtrusive. Headboards, on the other hand, are designed to give a decorative finishing touch to a bedroom scheme, as well as serving a practical purpose, but don't make them too elaborate.

Bed manufacturers seem never to have seen the need to make the base of the bed look attractive. In fact, they appear to go out of their way to upholster the divan base and mattress in the ugliest, most prominent fabrics they can find – and this is where valances can have a useful role to play.

Valances should be as near invisible as you can make them. There are various ways of achieving this. One is to make a valance in exactly the same fabric as the bed hangings and bedspread, and treat the valance fabric in the same way as the other bedroom furnishings. This effectively turns the upholstery of the bed into a coherent whole. Generally, if the bed is frilly, the valance should be too; if it is in a simpler style, keep the valance in sympathy. But, in general, the less flounce the better. It is

also a good idea, if the bed hangings pick up a colour in the carpet, to edge the bottom end of the valance in this shade. By this means the carpet is also incorporated in the scheme.

A second way to hide the valance is to make it entirely in the same shade as the carpet, especially if this is a dark one. In this case, the fabric should be as plainly tailored as possible with only a single pleat at each corner. This works best when the base of the bed is low – there would be too much fabric altogether if the same scheme were applied to a high Victorian bed – which, anyway, would probably look fine with no valance. Other antique beds can also stand alone.

Another suggestion is to pretend that the valance is something else entirely. You could hide the bed base with, say, dull black velvet and above that add a faux leopard skin throw diagonally so that the bulk of the base was hidden; this same scheme would work with any dark base half-covered with a fabric to match the curtains or hangings. The stronger fabric would draw the eye and the dark background would recede. Experiment and see.

ABOVE A simple, if antique, single bed has a matching quilt and headboard in a pretty red and white print. The valance beneath is a Regency stripe of the same shades and period.

RIGHT This is a stylist's dream of a bedroom, where everything (even the books) matches the blue and white scheme. Yet it was achieved on a tight budget with tea towels for the valances.

OPPOSITE PAGE, ABOVE LEFT White is perfect for bed linen – but it doesn't have to be plain white. It can be embroidered, damask, appliquéd or, as here, have an integral pattern woven in.

OPPOSITE PAGE, BELOW LEFT Valances are best when they don't try to make statements. Leave the pleating simple and tend towards colours which vanish into the carpet or floor.

OPPOSITE PAGE, RIGHT The severe lines of American half-tester beds are made comfortable by the addition of large, comfy pillows against the hard wooden headboards. Always make beds comfortable for lounging on as well as sleeping in.

BELOW A cotton headboard is neatly piped in matching fabric to make an abstract pattern. Bed linen has been carefully chosen to emphasize it.

RIGHT Padded satins at the head and foot of the bed make for a look reminiscent of Hollywood in the 1930s. The valance is kept utterly plain, as is the cotton-upholstered footstool at the base.

FAR RIGHT, BOTTOM A painted wooden edge surrounds an upholstered headboard to give a strong line to the shape. The mix of steel grey wood, white headboard and bright pink cushions is highly effective.

RIGHT Walls of white silk have been padded in a bedroom to give the effect of panelling. The vertical lines make patterns in an otherwise plain room.
BELOW Padded walls are an excellent way of softening acoustics and reducing noise from outside. The walls are silk and the hangings soft cotton.

In contrast with valances, headboards should be charming and decorative and chosen cunningly to complement the bed itself. If a headboard is upholstered, the fabric should allude to, but not necessarily match, the counterpane or quilt – a check matched with a stripe perhaps or a chintz picking up a plain colour. If it is your intention to pile up cushions or pillows against the headboard, keep the board simple so that it doesn't fight with the cushions or pillows but acts as a background against which to display them.

On a practical note, remember that headboards can get grubby and must therefore be designed for easy cleaning. Personally – because it is not easy to clean upholstered headboards – I would be inclined to stick with wood or metal bedheads (or fabric ones, if you must) and make mounds of cushions do the work instead.

The purpose of a headboard is not only to make the bed look decorative and furnished but to create a comfortable backing for people who like to lounge or read in bed. Since we all go about this in different ways – slumping or bolt upright, veered to one side or another or hardly visible above the bed clothes – a pile of cushions is far more adaptable. Cover them in fabrics which match or complement the rest of the bedroom and pile them up in front of the regular, white-covered pillows. Round bolsters and square French pillows make excellent stuffings.

Another idea is to make overstuffed pillows or cushions with ties and secure them to the bed head with bows. These, again, can be upholstered in the same fabrics as the curtains or counterpane but have the advantage of being easily removable for washing.

accessories

As well as the grand productions of soft furnishings – the sofas and the curtains, the quilts and hangings – there are quantities of fabric accessories in every house. They deserve equal consideration because getting these details wrong messes up the whole. Once you have decided on the overall feel of a room, you will know how to angle the details. The way to achieve a satisfactory result is to stick to the appropriate – shells by the sea, ferns in the conservatory, 18th-century Arcady in the Georgian drawing room.

If you are aiming for an all-white, pared-down style of bedroom, your laundry bag on the door should not attract attention to itself, but you may be able to soften the whole with a tower of subtle silk boxes or a single Japanese screen on a wall or in a corner. An 18th-century living room would demand a different screen, in a toile or pictorial fabric; while frilly gingham lampshades will add charm to a cottage kitchen; and a tablecloth patterned with shells or guinea-fowl feathers will dress up a fisherman's hide or a garden bothy. Accessories can be used to make slight modifications to a room. Suppose you have a basic blue and white chintzy bedroom and you

buy a Japanese red lacquer tray – while not enough to make a statement, it indicates a direction you'd like to pursue. Add to the red of the tray a similar pair of bags hanging on the back of a door and an indigo kimono with red stripes from a hanger. Instantly, the room adopts an East/West axis.

If your garden room is looking too greenhousy, give the lamps fabric shades of a white-background chintz decorated with ivy leaves or geranium flowers. Never neglect apparently insignificant details: white damask napkins in a formal dining room, old-fashioned knitted dishcloths by the butler's sink, a series of boxes covered in a John Stefanides turquoise and white

LEFT The antique air of the damask undercloth on this upholstered table is quietly emphasized by a white cotton sheet thrown over the top. The zig-zag cutouts have a heraldic feel about them.
BELOW A cotton table cover is rigorously folded and hung to floor level to show off the wooden floor and bordered matching mats. The bright green grasses in terracotta pots and the baskets on the table hint at a scheme that is subtly oriental.

OPPOSITE PAGE, LEFT Robust striped mattress ticking covers a plain coathanger, and the whole is tied with darker ribbons.
OPPOSITE PAGE, RIGHT A length of plain ribbon, wound around a frame, creates a pretty lampshade. At the bottom, braid adds decoration. The lampshade is simple to make and gives you the flexibility to introduce a subtle splash of colour to a room.

LEFT A small footstool is covered in a dark velvet which has been imprinted with gold chequers to suit its shape. The nearby sofa is covered in textured silk.
BELOW Fabric mounted to make elegant screens can be used to hide or divide a difficult room and, as here, be carefully lit for maximum interest.

print of dolphins behind the office desk and a matching fabric-covered pot for pencils by the telephone. You could even patronize one particular fabric designer and buy his or her designs to make your own accessories, from padded slippers and matching dressing gown to personal bound folders (a bookbinder will make them) for filing and squares to use as tray cloths and napkins. Those to watch include Cath Kidston, with her flowery evocations, Bennison's tea-stained florals and Andrew Martin's jokey animals. Or take period fabrics to mix and match, such as toile de Jouy, French tickings or William Morris's complex designs, which must surely be due for a revival.

OPPOSITE PAGE Patchwork was once the preserve of paupers using up scraps of fabric. Raid sample boxes and scrap bins from tweed mills to get this charming, winter effect.
RIGHT This handsome tan leather basket holds towels and blankets in a bedroom. Leather is heavy, so don't buy big leather baskets to carry around.

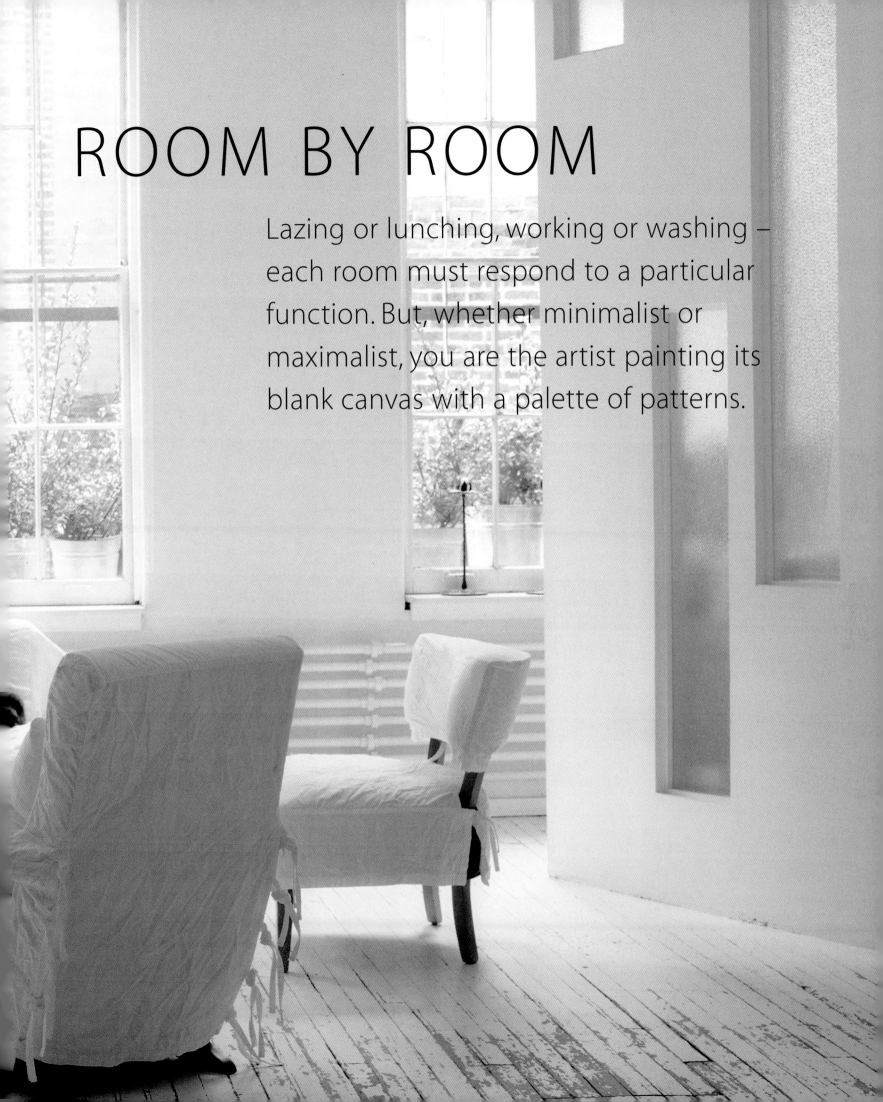

ROOM BY ROOM

Lazing or lunching, working or washing – each room must respond to a particular function. But, whether minimalist or maximalist, you are the artist painting its blank canvas with a palette of patterns.

living rooms

The living room is the most important room in the house from the point of view of design. This is where you and your friends will have the leisure and chance to appreciate how you live, what you enjoy and what statements you wish to make about yourself. In the 18th century, drawing rooms were stiff and formal places where chairs were ranked back against the walls and moved into groupings when families and friends were visiting. There was no sense of relaxation about them. In the 19th century, fixed groups of chairs and tables appeared – but so did the formal parlour, which was used only for grand affairs, such as a visit by the vicar.

As the 19th century progressed, living rooms became so cluttered – by chairs, tables with cloths, pictures and vases stuffed with peacock feathers – that it became almost impossible to move about them. Drawing rooms and parlours were intended to boost a family's status by parading the best (as much of it as possible) that the owner could offer. The ostentation was designed to make it clear to which class the householder belonged and how much wealth he could boast.

As class has become less of an indicator of an individual's place in the world, style has taken its place and living rooms are where style is paraded, even shown off. This is the room were we are most likely to make a statement about ourselves – what type of furniture and painting we like, our family values and our conspicuous consumption. A further element in

OPPOSITE PAGE Two impressive modern abstracts are allowed to dominate this quietly luxurious day room because the dark carpet and taupe chairs with their cream throws lead the eye towards the pictures on the wall. So does the white pottery.
ABOVE LEFT Rich earthy suede on the day bed is echoed in the cushions and lamp base. The lampshade is made of silk to tone with the sheer curtains.
LEFT Padded cushions, neatly upholstered in dark suede, mean that this low table can be adapted into a stool.

LEFT Voile fabric behind an internal glass wall divides in half this severe New York living room. The softly coloured sofas are covered in wool and given silken cushions.
RIGHT A completely different colour scheme is used in the same room (see left) with its bright red chairs and cotton flowery cushions on a cotton-covered sofa.

the mix is that the world of fashion has been advancing steadily into the area of interior design to the extent that, by the end of the 1990s, the two had become inextricably linked. Think of the frequent shots in magazines of the newest interiors combined with models lounging about on sofas in relaxing clothes (detailed in the captions along with the wallpaper and curtain fabric). The idea is to offer people a complete lifestyle in their living rooms, with rough linen curtains designed to mix and match with rough linen kimonos and drawstring trousers. Design firms such as Manuel Canovas and Monkwell, as well as fashion designers with 'home' ranges, are bringing out new collections once or twice a year, and we are supposed to adjust our rooms to follow these passing fashions.

My advice is to watch what is happening and adjust the minutiae but to take the whole with a vast pinch of salt. Just as fashions return after a generation's gap, so do fabrics and the way we use them. Some of the most loved interiors are those where the owners have refused to change with changing fashion but kept the style that they personally liked. Among them are grand country houses where the original 18th- and 19th-century curtains, rugs, cushions and hangings are still in place, Art Nouveau interiors, such as

that at the National Trust's Wightwick Hall, near Wolverhampton, and Parisian salons where Art Deco still survives. These interiors are impossible to fake and their value is beyond that of any fad or fashion.

If you are designing a living room from scratch, it is nevertheless a good idea to consider what's currently in, while bearing in mind that one day it will be out – and nothing looks less appealing than a highly unfashionable living room. Even if you turn your back on fashion and decide to go for a traditional room, remember that, after a while, you may change your mind. Design the space in such a way that the most expensive or basic elements will not date while the accessories can be updated whenever you want or can afford it. These accessories are, of course, the soft furnishings – which anyway have a life far shorter than furniture, fireplaces or paintings.

However hard you try to avoid it, the fabrics and furnishings in your living room give clues about the kind of person you are. Are you traditional, with a liking for chintz and antiques, or authentic, searching out textiles that have been copied exactly from those of the 17th or 18th century? Are you minimal and neutral, surrounded by fabrics in colours such as chalk and string, or vibrantly

LEFT If you are fortunate enough to have parquet flooring of good quality along with interesting panelling, it makes sense to give less emphasis to the upholstery. In this room, the sofa is low-key compared with the architecture.
BELOW Everything in this generous living room has been colour coordinated – but so cleverly that it looks almost natural. Blond wood on the floors and in the tables emphasizes the amber shades of the upholstery. Even the logs match the whole.

LEFT The oriental feel of this living room derives not only from the objects and the table but from the kimono-patterned mixture of cushions on the inviting window seat, which is itself upholstered in a slubbed Thai silk.

ethnic, with kilims on the walls and pashminas on the sofa? The answer is probably reflected in the clothes you wear: if you dress in classics, you will want a straightforward room; if you go for BoHo, it will be bright finds from antique markets and thrift shops; if you cannot live without a label, then you'll look at the home collections of Ralph Lauren, Nicole Farhi and Donna Karan.

Comfort yourself with the thought that, if you had a completely clear mind, you would never manage to negotiate the vast quantities of fabrics and styles on offer. The proliferation of choice has been made worse by the onrush of communications. People travel the world looking for ethnic fabrics woven in the heart of Africa or dyed in the foothills of the Himalayas. Collections from all continents are piled high in swatch books in the major stores, and the auction houses increase their textile sales yearly. A firm in Nepal recently contacted me through the internet offering a collection of pashmina throws in more than 1000 colours.

For a start, it makes sense not to go against a house's original architectural style. Although it is possible to transform a Victorian artisan's cottage into a traditional Japanese interior, not only will this take a great deal of effort (hiding the walls with translucent paper screens, covering the floors in tatami), but also it will seem ludicrous to anyone with a sense of place. So, if you have a Victorian artisan's cottage, copy the style of a Victorian artisan. This doesn't mean that you have to be totally authentic. You can use styles from the 1950s or the Art Deco 1920s, but it is crucial that the scale is right. Those 'contemporary' fabrics with abstract shapes and primary colours that appeared after the Second World War are fine as long as the size of the pattern is in sympathy with the size of the window.

Today's fashionable loft and warehouse spaces demand something on a grand scale. You could try a large toile de Jouy pattern or an Indonesian batik in such an apartment, but don't skimp on the fabric. Curtains should hang from

RIGHT A country room with a modern twist concentrates on plain white shapes with only three checked red cushions to add colour and pattern.
OPPOSITE PAGE A clever eye has used an Indian kilim to match the American Indian fabrics of this Santa Fe scheme. Red is the only strong colour in this room.

LEFT People who collect interesting antiques, such as these bird houses and cages, want their finds to stand out. In such a situation, you can subordinate the furnishing fabrics to the objects by picking colours in similar shades but a tone softer.

ABOVE Virtually every fabric in this room – from the kilim on the floor to the checked blinds – is different. Yet clever mixing and matching of neutrals and blue provides cohesion. A swatch board is the way to control the colours.

the top of the window to the floor and be impressively ebullient. I have seen one such loft space designed as though it were a drawing room in a stately home, and it worked well – as does the notion of setting up the whole as a Scottish shooting lodge with tartan curtains, carpet and cushions piled high on vast sofas.

Richard Rogers and other top London architects have regularly taken 18th-century town houses and transformed them into plain white interiors. Even the ornate cornices and stately fireplaces fit in well with plain white curtains, cushionless chairs, sofas in neutral cambric and rugless wooden floors. Minimalism needs both discipline and the willingness to spend a lot of money on the few furnishings

on show. Those white curtains must be the best. Other designers have successfully made traditional English living rooms into celebrations of African or Chinese style by using the other countries' fabrics in a classical European way. A painted piece of Chinese silk turned into a curtain bridges the two cultures, while African textiles in stark shades – umber, terracotta, black and ochre – can hang comfortably on a wall behind a plain-coloured European sofa.

Just as the way in which you tie a scarf can make you look smart or dated, so will the way you marshal your cushions and your throws. One year, a throw will lie in a heap, as though casually dropped on a chair; the next, it will be neatly folded over the chair's arm. Cushions divide and multiply: sometimes there are dozens piled high into fabric mountains; at other times they will be in a neat tower block in subtle shades. Quilts appear in the living room before being exiled to the bedroom once again, while tables may be completely concealed by cloths that reach to the carpet or revealed with nothing but a small antique embroidered napkin under a plant pot. You don't have to follow these shifts slavishly – indeed, you should not – but you should be aware of them.

Similarly, watch out for shifts in colour schemes. Living rooms may ask for bright contrasts – I always remember that of a famous art critic who mixed bright citrus walls with stunning scarlet curtains in his Yorkshire manor house – or they may lean towards the subfusc. The current passion is for subtle and natural earth colours, which can be found everywhere from seaside cottages to Manhattan penthouses. Shades achieved with vegetable dyes, always less abrasive than the chemical ones, are also popular, which explains the crossover of indigo from jeans to curtains and the long reign of toiles in madders and ochres.

Consciously or subconsciously, we are following a politically green line. Earth tones seem natural, ecologically sound and caring – yes, even in decor, politics plays a part. Another explanation for their popularity is that these colours are calm and soft and we find them relaxing after work. Also, these shades generally appear in the type of fabrics that ask to be snuggled into: velvets, fleeces, rough wools, handwoven cottons and cashmeres, which are soft to the touch and drape luxuriously. Some of us imagine using our living rooms for long lazy weekends with friends – lounging on sofas in linen daytime pyjamas and cashmere espadrilles, eating fusion food from Eastern ceramics and admiring a spiky modernist flower arrangement while snuggling into a pashmina throw.

Your dream may be different. The Dutch interiors of painters such as Vermeer may have made you lust after the heavy plain curtains that sweep the tiled floors of the Amsterdam houses, or you may see in the paintings of Matisse a carefree Mediterranean window decked with Stefanides curtains of a Grecian blue, framing a vase full of bright anemones. You may see yourself with feet balanced on a Victorian embroidered footstool in front of a bright coal fire, above which is a Berlin woolwork picture. Or you may want to display the kind of eclectic mix that is found in townhouses from San Francisco to Berlin, where every cover is tailored and disciplined, and where clever lights pick the glitter from a single Indian embroidery. If you can get in touch with your own fantasy, it will fuel your inner vision.

RIGHT A simple neutral check on chairs and sofas works well for a country living room. More checks are visible in the cushions, throws and flat rug.
OPPOSITE PAGE Stripes both on the cabriole-legged chair and Roman blinds hold together a countrified living room in Connecticut. There are blues in the floral cushions while plain lime-green versions on a white sofa draw attention to the profusion of flowers and plants.

bedrooms

Unlike living rooms, bedrooms do not have to make statements to anyone but ourselves. Bedrooms are all about relaxation, comfort, feeling at ease with ourselves. They are, too, a launching pad for the day at the office, for an evening out or a weekend away, for a holiday or an imposing appearance at an important event. They are the store and warehouse for all our clothes, shoes, accessories, make-up and personal belongings and, quite often, linen cupboard, airing cupboard and route to the bathroom.

Bedrooms need to be highly organized behind the scenes. The clothes, accessories, bed linen and towels need to be there but not to be seen. The best bedrooms have a guileless air of calm, space and order. So, the first thing to decide when decorating a bedroom is how to conceal all these elements.

One option is to cover all the walls with cupboards and wardrobes – which will probably reduce the room's total dimensions by about two metres. If you have the space, this works well, especially if you can disguise some cupboards to resemble panelling, print rooms (rooms with prints stuck on the walls) or plain, papered walls, while giving others pretty glazed doors like Georgian windows with, behind them, simple ruched fabric to match or complement the bedroom curtains. This will, in effect, split up the walls without adding free-standing pieces of furniture to the

ABOVE AND RIGHT Bedrooms are growing increasingly formal – perhaps because they are used as refuges during the day as well as at night. This dark-chocolate bedcover is made of textured striped wool. The square pillows and cushions are in cream and bordered in the same chocolate shade.
OPPOSITE PAGE, BELOW Curtains over walls are a good way to disguise a small room. Generously box-pleated fabric in two neutral shades conceals this bedroom's dimensions (and lets you hide stuff behind them). Plain fabrics also help to increase the sense of space.

RIGHT A soft putty headboard is made of ribbed cotton, while the bedspread is a softer shade of ironed linen. Square pillows and lampshade are lighter still.

room. I've seen this idea succeed in stylish hotel suites where plain walls in Swedish green, rose-madder pink and Mediterranean blue are broken up by green gingham curtains, bed hangings and curtained glazed cupboards, by blue toile de Jouy or by a stylish flower or chinoiserie patterns in green and pink. Modernist rooms can repeat the same trick using a fabric version of the plain colour that is inevitably on the walls. Try, for instance, a white slubbed silk behind wardrobe doors to change the texture of a white wall, or use a near-black navy gent's worsted behind glass and for the curtains.

The skill in a bedroom is to achieve a stylish relaxed atmosphere without overdoing the flounces. Modern interiors are especially averse to matching valances, curtains, bed hangings, scatter cushions and padded

BELOW A welcoming London bedroom constrasts strongly figurative walls with a suede bedhead and multiple patterned cushions. The trimmed bedcover is of wool.
OPPOSITE PAGE Waffle-weave cotton is fairly easy to find, easy to wash and cheap to buy. What more could you want in a bedspread? If you could bear to change this charming room, you could cut it down into towels too.

coathangers. If you follow such a route, you risk looking out of place in your own bedroom unless you wear matching colours at all times. Avoid matching curtains with wallpaper – it makes a room seem curiously insubstantial, as though the walls were only as thick as the curtains.

When planning how to control the flounce factor, think about how you use your bedroom. Are you like Lady Diana Cooper, who stayed in bed until midday, dictating to her secretary, opening her post, stroking her little dog and taking the first social engagements of the day from under her pristine quilt? Do you, more prosaically, watch the television during the day and evening while reclining

on your bed rather than on a sofa in the living room? Do you like to make your bedroom a haven from the family – or, for that matter, from real life?

If any of these is the case, plenty of cushions around the bed is an excellent idea, as is a washable counterpane. When you want to lounge around during the day, the counterpane will give the room a slightly more formal look than rumpled sheets, and you can prop yourself up on a selection of smartly laundered cushions and pillows. Add to this a fire – probably the coal-and-gas-effect sort, unless you want to struggle upstairs with buckets of coal – and pretty tub chairs in loose covers beside it and you have

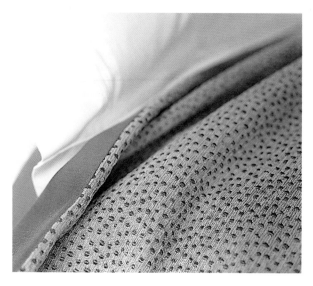

FAR LEFT The rippling pattern of the opalescent voile curtains is reflected in the circular moon mirror in a quiet bedroom. The textured silk bedcover has horizontal seam detailing.

FAR LEFT BELOW Plain white bedrooms are always cool and calm: a space to relax in at the end of the day. They also allow you to mix and match the colours of your clothes or to create patterns from them.

OPPOSITE PAGE, ABOVE RIGHT Small abstract prints make excellent bedcovers in modern or minimalist bedrooms. This cotton version provides texture as well as colour.

OPPOSITE PAGE, BELOW RIGHT The overscaled headboard of this bed is covered in soft suede, while the oriental table at its base has upholstered, darker leather cushions. These colours are picked up by the three colours of bed linen used.

BELOW This soothing bedroom with its wall of windows is in a converted Scottish cinema. The 17th-century oak chair has been emphasized by the complete self-effacement of the voile curtains and the white bed linen.

RIGHT In keeping with the rough timber and unplastered brick of a barn conversion, the fabrics on the bed are rough in texture and plain in colour.

your own boudoir or private living room. I don't exclude men from wanting their own private bedrooms – everyone needs to relax in private – but a male bedroom should exclude even a single flounce. One smart designer I know had to make do with a single bedsit when he started out. Apart from being immaculately tidy, he made special fabric boxes to slide under the high bed and created green baize screens ornamented with architectural prints to hide his clothes and office work. He went as far as having a large round table with a green baize tablecloth reaching down to the floor, and on this were magazines, books and a central large orchid. It was stunning.

Indeed, if space is limited, plain fabrics work wonders if complemented by walls of a slightly darker shade. All the colour can be concentrated in plain fabrics – curtains, cushions, screens, cupboards – while leaving ornaments to stay monochrome black and white. Fabrics such as baize and felt can even be stapled to the walls, both to provide a depth of colour and to improve the acoustics. On the cloth, you can staple or pin black and white prints in formal groups.

When you turn from urban bedrooms, which generally look inwards on themselves unless there's a particularly attractive roofscape, to country rooms, include the view in the general scheme. It was in the 18th century that designers realized that not only should all rooms look out on fine landscapes but also that the landscape should be changed to suit the view from the window.

To create the best view possible, consider the bedroom window as part of the scenery. This means that your curtains should be at one with what is outside. This doesn't have to mean a floral or foliage pattern, but the colours should lead the eye on. Black, for example, would be a sad choice because its effect would be to intrude on the view beyond and block it off, while exuberant scarlets and yellows also impose themselves rather than leading the eye on. Blues of all shades match the sky, greens recede towards the leaves and grass, while white, especially in a fine fabric, is both neutral and encouraging for the sunlight. If, in winter, this pastoral idyll usually turns into a white hell of gales and snow, consider adding heavy, dark curtains to cut your bedroom off from the elements and add a sense of warm security.

If you are lucky – or clever – enough to have a four-poster in the bedroom, make the most of it. The bed will always be the room's focal point so it is worth spending time and money to get the hangings right. If you

ABOVE Very simple schemes in a bedroom allow you to adapt to changes in fashion both of decor and of clothes (which are an important element of any bedroom). Here the Chinese slippers are very much part of the design.
LEFT Family photographs make up the pattern in this modern print-room bedroom but the colour comes from a single note of brilliant aquamarine. You can often achieve the best results by being bold.
OPPOSITE PAGE Fashion-conscious folk might like to leave the colour in the bedroom to the clothes they wear. All-white fabrics and duck-egg wall in this room allow the clothes to keep the upper hand.

can't afford to spend hundreds on just the right fabric, it is possible to economize by making the bed's linings, headboard and tailored top in a plain fabric that picks out a single colour of the expensive fabric used for the outer curtains and hangings around the top frame. In the 18th century, they were extremely clever at finding linings with tiny patterns to complement the important fabric, and some decorators or textile firms with their own collections still make unobtrusive all-over patterns to use

purely as linings. These little charmers can also turn up on the bed's piled cushions, on the linings of the curtains and behind glazed doors. Even the laundry bags can match because the advantage of the tiny all-over design is that it is the most modest of textiles.

Country bedrooms can also absorb more clutter than those in the town. I'm keen, here, on piles of fabric boxes, from those large enough to take extra pillows and blankets to small boxes for jewellery, make-up, linen handkerchiefs and extra buttons. It's smart if these boxes pick up references to other fabrics used in the room, but smarter still if you can vary the patterns slightly so that some boxes match the curtains, others match its lining, some are a single plain shade and others a stripe. Stick with high-quality wooden coathangers, all exactly the same. Although this sounds pernickety, it makes it easier to organize your wardrobe and will encourage you to colour-code your clothes on the rail. Even if no one but you sees it, the knowledge of a well-planned wardrobe will encourage tidiness everywhere in the bedroom.

Bedrooms may be the hardest rooms to keep under control, but, if you give plenty of thought to the fabrics, textures and patterns right from the start, it will make tidiness easy – even enjoyable. Once everything has its place – drawers, boxes, bags and covers all just the right size; blankets, linen, cushion and duvet covers piled type by type on adequate shelves; and the bed and furniture positioned to catch the early sun or the perfect view – you will find that being there is such a pleasure that tidiness becomes second nature.

ABOVE This charming country bedroom is virtually all red and white – but with striped, checked, pictorial and toile materials all jostling for attention. Apart from a single touch of blue, the rest is in soothing neutrals.
RIGHT This traditional American look is easily copied. A pretty quilt has its blue and white colours picked up by the pillows and cushions. An upright chair has been painted to tone.
OPPOSITE PAGE As an alternative to buying from a single designer, you can also find colours and fabrics to complement each other by buying from a single country market. These stripes, checks and traditional patterns came from the market in Tangier.

kitchens and dining rooms

I keep reading that the dining room is dead. Not for me, it isn't. While I do eat in other rooms, the dining room is the one I like best. It's here where proper meals are eaten, the room which is best set up for making the most of food. At the same time, I am starting to think that using the kitchen for meals is the last thing I want to do – almost as bad as eating in an office, relaxing in the room which is really intended for work.

The place where you normally eat should be as much defined as the place where you work, bathe or read. We don't expect offices, bathrooms and libraries suddenly to change into cosy, candlelit areas – nor should we expect kitchens suddenly to become conducive to eating or, for that matter, dining rooms to be suitable for cooking. Even if the two, because of circumstances, have to be in the same space, they should be clearly delineated.

From the soft furnishing point of view, kitchens are a near-disaster area. Assuming that you actually cook rather than just open packets there, curtains, blinds, cushions and floor coverings are likely to become infiltrated with grease, cabbage-scented steam and other unhappy cooking smells. I don't think you should keep any fabrics in the near neighbourhood of the hot plates and ovens other than oven gloves, aprons, tea towels and washing-up cloths, unless you are willing to wash them every week.

LEFT What other curtains could there possibly be in this rustic room but gingham? However unimportant in the whole scheme, every element absolutely must chime in with the rest.
ABOVE Linen, today a luxury fabric, is notable for its creasing, which gives added texture. Here a crumpled plain cloth hides the sink.

LEFT In a room as apparently basic as this French kitchen, the storage cupboards are screened with neutral hessian, which is heavy enough to hang in perfect gathers. Simple fabric curtains used to hide kitchen paraphernalia are ideal in country kitchens where the family also eats. Materials soften the acoustics and make a working room more friendly.

BELOW Why have expensive fitted cupboard doors in your kitchen when a pretty frilled check curtain will hide the gubbins just as well? But make sure the curtains are always perfectly clean.

ABOVE Perfect decorative touches make the difference between a room that looks acceptable and one that is stunning in its impact. The small strip of red and white gingham edging the inset shelf – and chosen to match the tea towel beneath – is a simple example of how it can be done.

RIGHT The simple linen tablecloth is striking for its sharply pressed creases.
BELOW RIGHT Overscaled checks upholster the 18th-century chairs, while the chaise longue has a similarly coloured ticking to match the colour of the panelled walls.
OPPOSITE PAGE Lots of checks and stripes always create an informal effect, even in this room with its panelling and colonial chandelier.

However, it is quite possible, in the sort of large basement you find in townhouses or the generous rooms of farmhouse kitchens, to divide the two areas successfully and, with the aid of room dividers and hoods over the oven and hotplates, to keep cooking smells confined to a small area around where the real work is being done. So, while the kitchen end of a room may be a fabric-free zone, the dining area can still sport heavy curtains, chair covers and the smartest of table linen.

Whether they are part of the kitchen or separate rooms, dining rooms need an element of formality. That is not to say that ancestors have to frown down on everyone or that the curtains should be figured velvet, but that fabrics should not take the emphasis away from the food. Dining rooms should make food look its best and be an aid to the digestion. Restaurants are an excellent source of inspiration. Any good restaurant will provide newly laundered, high-quality table linen. This may simply be napkins, with the table top made of wood, zinc or cleverly coloured synthetics, or the table may be covered with a simply coloured damask tablecloth. It, and the napkins, absolutely must be freshly laundered. No creases, no crumbs, no stains, no spills. Personally, I like both to be pure white, but I'm not dogmatic about this.

Restaurants also take great care to create a decorative style in their dining rooms that works both during the day and at night. This is not easy, but the colours, texture and weight of the curtains should be chosen to look good when either drawn apart or closed. Cushions on the upright chairs also need to chime in with the curtains and be intended to look comfortable but not obtrusive. And, while every dining-room chair should be squashy enough to last a full evening, it is just as important to make sure that people are at the right height to feel comfortable

when eating at the table. Dining tables vary considerably in their height, which can be disconcerting to guests.

Cushions should be anchored onto the chairs so that they cannot slip off while you are eating. Some dining chairs have drop-in seats which, happily, look formal while allowing even amateur upholsterers to change the cover of the seat as the decor changes. Country chairs are made with harder wooden seats, sometimes dished to give a touch more comfort. Frankly, they need the addition of a squashy cushion if your guests are to last the course. These can either be plonked on the chair, risking slipping off during the meal, or tied on around the chair back. If you choose the latter, make the tie as simple as possible – no room is helped by eight chairs with pussycat bows on their backs. Nor am I keen on case-covered chairs as flouncy as Victorian ladies in crinolines. If you want to buy cheap chairs and cover them, as they did in the 19th century, with cheap cotton cases, make them as simple and washable as you can, but this option may cost more than buying nice chairs in the first place.

Dining tables of any quality cost as much as a small car and few people want to splash out to this extent. The answer is, therefore, to find or to make a generously sized

table out of plywood or MDF (medium-density fibreboard) and cover it with a pretty cloth. If the legs are good, ensure that they stay visible; if they are simple trestles, cover the table at all times with the kind of moquette or chenille heavy cloth used by the Victorians. At meal times, add a plain white tablecloth or pretty cotton chosen to suit the permanent undercloth.

Few people bother any more with tablecloths, napkins or tray cloths, so there are lots of beauties to be discovered in antique shops. Look for top-quality damask napkins and tablecloths, or find lovingly embroidered sets done by Great Aunt Emily and thrown out by her ungrateful family. For the undercloth, search for paisley shawls that have worn out in the centre, thin kilims and oriental rugs (used for tablecloths in Tudor times) and fine silk curtains; since these undercloths will be protected by the real tablecloths, they will rarely need cleaning. Even a quilt looks splendid in this context.

If you are nervous that the dining area of the room will absorb cooking smells from the nearby kitchen, copy the clever idea devised by *World of Interiors*. Over a decade ago, a stylist found the factory that made all those glass cloths which have a 10cm (2in) broad red or blue stripe with the words 'Made in Ireland' and 'Glass Cloth' woven into it. She ordered metres of the stuff and used it to make cushion covers, napkins, tablecloths and

ABOVE The dark wood of this stylish dining chair has been softened by a pale upholstered cover that is echoed by the tablecloths. The chair's quasi-oriental design is emphasized by the use of a Japanese flower arrangement and Chinese dim sum boxes.
RIGHT AND FAR RIGHT This dining room exemplifies how a good eye can create a sophisticated effect from inexpensive and disparate elements. Multicoloured chair seats and tablecloths all have touches of grass green, which are pointed up by the green crockery.

curtains. It looked both crisp and sophisticated and could be washed every week. Similarly, Roger Banks-Pye of Colefax – who was passionate about blue and white – bought a whole pile of matching blue and white checked table napkins and had them sewn up into curtains.

With some ingenuity, it is possible to find fabrics that actually enjoy being washed at least once a month, and even benefit from it. Think, for example, of blue denim, the printed African indigo batik that fades and softens with washing. and everything from ticking to dishcloths to floor cloths that are intended to soak up the dirt and enjoy it.

Both kitchens and dining rooms allow us plenty of licence. Kitchens are working rooms that need no flossing up. The equipment, recipe books, colour ingredients and plain metal pans provide all the colour and excitement a room needs. Any cushions or curtains should be in keeping with the purpose of making good food. A dining room is more like a theatrical setting, designed for impact. Even modernist dining rooms can benefit from a study of how they were in the past. Fabric colours were chosen with candlelight in mind (even if it's now electricity on a dimmer switch) and the type and textures were those that reflected the glow and added to it. Textiles that improved the acoustics were always preferred, whether they were carpets, tapestries or napped fabrics such as velvet or moquette.

If the style you have adopted in a dining area does not make you and your guests feel comfortable, by definition it's not stylish either.

ABOVE LEFT The two-toned blue stripe upholstery of these chairs is made of a short-pile velvet.
BELOW The chair seats are upholstered in cotton with a slight slub. Double piping shows attention to fine detail.

LEFT AND ABOVE Off-white fabrics are used for both curtains and chair covers for a Parisian monochrome setting. The wooden walls, chairs, table and shelves are dark brown. The lampshades are of silk and also off-white.
OPPOSITE PAGE Six stylish chairs in a classical Grecian style are covered with a broad horizontal stripe and set around a table that is totally covered in mouse-brown felt.

bathrooms

Giuseppe di Lampedusa's *The Leopard*, set in a Sicilian palazzo, first made me want a splendid bathroom; visits to Italy increased the longing. Luxuriously simple, Italian bathrooms have acres of marble – red, white, grey or green – along with pure-white waffle towels, bathmats, robes and slippers. That is really all a bathroom needs – especially if the walk-in shower is the size of a small room and the bathtub is adequate for a medium-sized hippopotamus.

ABOVE Bright yellow cotton curtains not only give a bathroom privacy but provide colour in an otherwise all-white scheme.
OPPOSITE PAGE These bathroom curtains are sewn with tiny shells (a job for the long winter nights), while the choice of soft lavender for towels and gown brings out a similar shade in the opalescent glass.
RIGHT Not just a bathroom, this is a place to lounge, with a cotton-covered chair and footstool plus a gold leather chair by the basin.

Bathrooms should always look fresh. This means that they should have good-quality clean linen in carefully chosen colours, and the towels should come in all sizes for guests, because people are surprisingly fussy about the size of towel they prefer for any one job. Towels should always appear new. While it is tempting to carry on with a set whose middle has lost its nap and whose edges have frayed to tassels – don't. Bath towels, even in good cotton and linen, are pretty cheap unless you insist on designer ware. Drape a couple of towels over a hot rail and pile the others up in tempting heaps for later use.

Unless you have a bathroom fit for an Italian palazzo, the space will frequently get steamy, so make sure that more permanent fabrics can be regularly washed. Plain cotton curtains, perhaps with a waffle texture reminiscent

of towels, are probably the best bet, while blinds are good (as long as they can be sponged) because they give you the opportunity to put attractive scent bottles and items of make-up on the windowsill.

If you have a large bathroom, you can have lots of fun. I especially like a bathroom with a rolltop bath in the centre, which allows you to arrange the rest of the space like a charming living room. Cane furniture covered with pretty, easily laundered cushions is perfect for lounging, throwing clothes over or relaxing in a huge towel after a bath. In this type of bathroom, allow yourself long chintzy curtains that match the cushions along with inner swathes of white voile to give a charming country look. Bathrooms of this size can survive a few flounces, especially if the room has a view over the countryside. I am not in favour of too much fuss around the walls – no

ABOVE Shower and bath curtains are always a problem because of the constant moisture. A simple white fabric is used here – but decoratively tied when not in use.
LEFT A thoroughly inviting sofa at the foot of the bath breaks down the boundaries between living area and bathroom.
OPPOSITE PAGE Understated use of grand fabrics makes this bathroom the height of luxury. The blond curtains and cushions, detailed with matching braid, are deliberately the same shade as the soft carpet and the wood panels surrounding the bath.

floral-painted tiles, please, or tiles with gloopy fish or 1970s geometric patterns. The patterns should be left to the fabrics you use. This should start with a simple bathmat or two, always washable, to cover an uncarpeted floor (fitted carpets are best avoided in the bathroom) and work up to accessories such as laundry bags. If you have several bathrooms in your house or apartment, it's a good idea to have the same colour theme in all of them because this will reduce the number of towels and accessories you need and make regular washing much easier.

Many houses also have bathrooms and cloakrooms intended for handwashing or use by guests rather than full-scale bathing. These need the same meticulous care, although they can be decorated with more daring. I know one collector who filled a downstairs cloaks with stuffed animals in glass cases and another who had letters written to him by royalty framed and hung on the walls – which goes to show that this sort of room can be themed. It is a place to hang jumble-sale buys such as guest towels with finely tatted edges and old school laundry bags; you can make it like a 1950s room with curtains with abstract shapes as decoration or imagine that this is part of the servants' hall or Shaker lodging house, with institutional white tiles, huckaback towels and curtains made of old tea towels that mark a royal jubilee. Seaside bathrooms may be decked with shells, loofahs, pumice stones and piles of sponges along with curtains patterned with sailing ships or seabirds' feathers. I have even seen a bathroom in open-plan style whose walls were made of tightly flexed blue-and-white-striped canvas.

While most modern bathrooms double as lavatories, there was a fashion in the 1950s and 1960s to separate the two. Even the tiniest lavatory can be given an element of fun – from curtains adorned with dinosaurs or prints of lions and tigers to zebra-skin floor rugs, chinoiserie light-pulls or chintzy fabrics whose ferny patterns match real fern houseplants.

Even in the smallest spaces, such amusing elements can be extended to tiny cabin bathrooms on yachts and in caravans or the rounded turrets of castles where the garderobe is traditionally situated. You can imitate the houses of the Landmark Trust, whose bathrooms vary from a circular space inspired by a Gothic tower to one that requires crossing an open roof in your dressing gown. Take time to choose appropriate details down to the last flannel that matches the toothmug and the soapdish in period and style. It's great fun to track down Gothic-style fabrics (Timney and Fowler is a useful source) to suit the arched windows, the basin and ewer and wooden towel rail found buried in a junk shop.

So, while bathrooms should remain relatively austere in atmosphere, there is plenty of research and sourcing to be done to make the most of even the smallest, steamiest space.

BELOW In a minimalist bathroom, divided from a single-roomed flat, a touch of luxury comes with the hanging lantern. This is an area whose effect relies solely on shape and texture.

LEFT This bathroom, in a one-room home, is divided from the rest of the living area by soft voile curtains. Yet it is so decorative that it could well by displayed when not in use. **OPPOSITE PAGE AND ABOVE RIGHT** A gigantic towel horse is used to screen a rolltop bath with heavy white cotton. It will act as a shower curtain and draught excluder as well as softening a large, simple bathroom. No towel horse actually comes in this size, but it's easily made. Then it can be used not only to drape protective heavy cotton around the bath but to hang a selection of colourful towels.

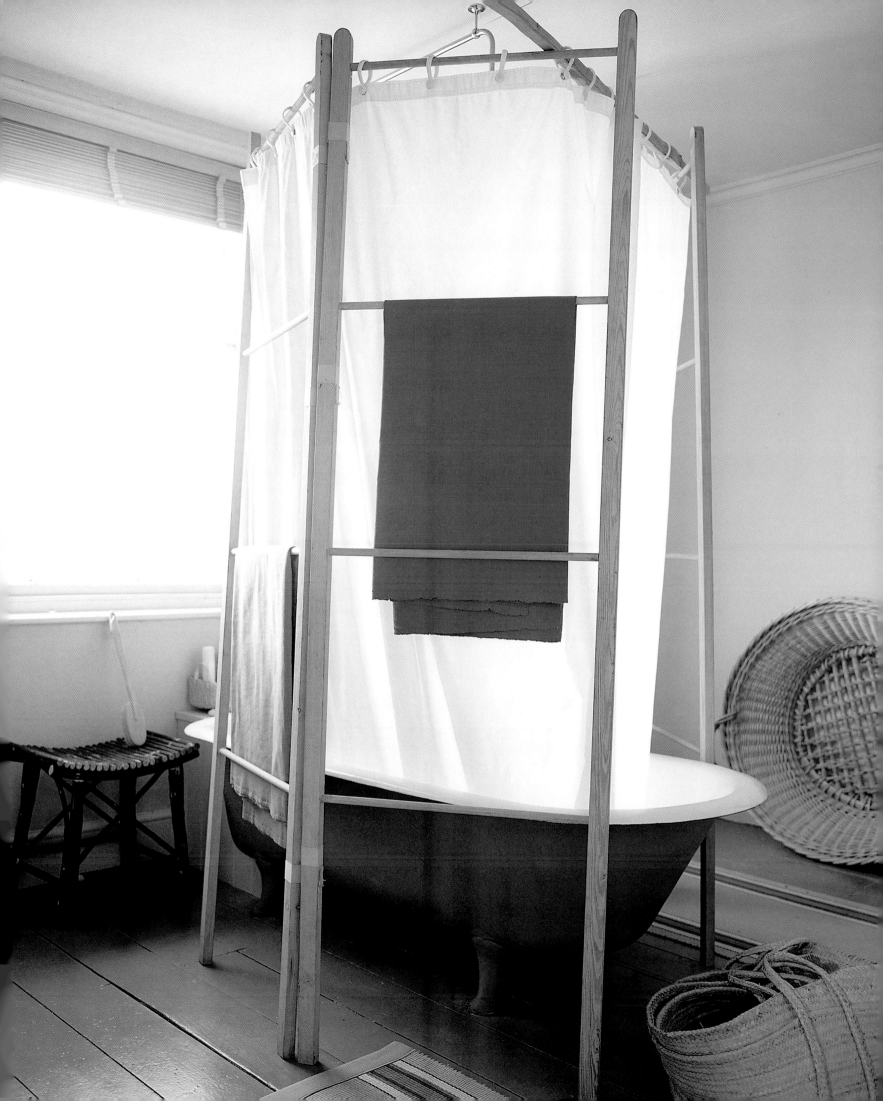

halls and landings

The main rooms of a house or apartment always get the most attention, but there are other spaces that need thought and imagination. If you live in a townhouse, whether in London, New York, Amsterdam or Edinburgh, the vital link with each room and each storey is the staircase hall. If you have a larger property, it is the entrance hall that creates the first impression, and all those corner landings can be transformed into anything from a favourite sun-filled sitting place to a relaxed home office. Equally, box rooms, attics under the eaves, disused larders and attached outhouses can, with skill, be made into some of the most important rooms in the house.

While the large rooms in a house are there for the major events of the day, the smaller rooms add character and charm, and the staircase and hall are the areas that pull the whole thing together. People frequently forget that a house should be treated as a whole entity, with each decorative scheme being connected with the next – and the stairs are the place where that trick can be performed. On the whole, the decorative scheme of a hall, landing or stairway should

be a lower-key version of what the rest of the decor is about. That is not to say it cannot be flamboyant – you can get away with stronger stripes, brighter colours and more theatrical effects in a hall than in a living room – but halls and stairways should encourage a sense of anticipation so that, when you reach the main rooms, you feel excited rather than let down. Halls and stairs should therefore be rather simple in their effect. They need few curtains, but those that are there should all be the same; the stair carpet should resemble that in an art gallery – classy but monotone – and any decorative flourishes should be saved for the rooms themselves.

In a five-storey townhouse, for instance, it is possible to have the carpet dark grey, the deep Georgian windows curtained with black and white toile. and to signal changes in design by changing the type of pictures as each floor is reached. The hallway may have black and white classical prints, while the walls bordering the stairs leading up to the next floor have great blocks of coloured 18th-century prints, which in turn give way to modern abstracts. Thus, while the basic decorative scheme involves the minimum number of colours, you get a sense that the rooms leading off will be surprisingly varied.

More generous houses have more generous landings on each floor, and these can be turned into small havens of comfort and style. I remember a charming house I visited in Bath where one landing had a large bureau bookcase in front of heavy tapestry curtains. The chair beside the desk was upholstered in a pretty matching fabric, and the whole area was hung with large 18th-century prints of birds. This was the owner's office, where a large window looked

OPPOSITE PAGE, ABOVE Stairways and halls often need curtains to keep out draughts and to make sense of a scheme that involves walls, stairs and windows. This elegant velvet curtain has appliquéd geometric patches to match the shape of the curtain heading.
OPPOSITE PAGE, BELOW LEFT AND RIGHT When decorating a hall, you don't need to bother about a source of light for reading or eating. Go for effect instead. These heavy curtains complement the wallpaper, chair cover and carpet. A curtain detail shows how a floral border has been used to link the plain and floral elements of the scheme.
RIGHT A sunny sitting area has been created in a traditional landing bay window. The blue and white check cushions don't quite match the curtains – which makes the whole area more relaxed.

BELOW Deep-buttoned cushion covers pad this fitted Chippendale-style corner bench, while cream-striped cushions are bordered in black. In a monochrome scheme the abstract cushion patterns are highly effective.

BELOW RIGHT A dark tan suede covers a padded cushion on a sunny window seat and the same leather is used for a decorative trimming to the blind. The design on the cushions replicates a 17th-century embroidery.

out on the long garden behind the house. It was beautifully decorated, strategically placed for callers and had one of the most attractive views in the whole building.

It is often the case that a small corner has the best morning sunlight or the most charming view in a house. Make the most of the space as a private breakfast room, a sunny place for a glass of wine at midday in winter, or a tiny sitting area to be kept for your exclusive use.

A landing or odd corner can be treated as a separate room with its own pretty curtains and cushions (which, because the area is bound to be small, can be exquisite). You can even mark out the territory by using a colour scheme for walls, floor and fabrics which is different from, but allied to, the decorative scheme of the passage or stairway. You can also, in this sort of area, increase the comfort factor by adding more cushions, paintings and rugs than would be normal in such a space.

OPPOSITE PAGE A choice of luscious fabrics in near-clashing reds and pinks transforms a potentially stark hallway into an exotic and inviting part of the house.

outdoors

Despite their unreliable climate, one of the keenest outdoor nations are the Swedes, who have thriving pavement cafés to greet the late sun and summer houses by the dozen around the lakes and inlets of Stockholm. Indeed, to achieve an exciting outdoor style, we might just as well take ideas from Scandinavia as from the traditional Mediterranean outdoor rooms, where heavy vines and wisterias are planted to shade brilliantly blue-coloured loggias and patios.

ABOVE Floral fabrics are ideal for cushions in the garden. **RIGHT** Canework chairs and sofas have loose-fitted cushions and backs made of old cotton checks, stripes and florals. Although it is roofed, this clapboarded patio forms an outdoor room.

Outdoor rooms, and semi-outdoor spaces such as conservatories and garden rooms, should be considered as extra living and dining rooms. It is here that we can entertain large parties for lunch, smart tea or supper under the stars; it's here that children most enjoy themselves and where, on lazy weekends, we can sit all day, from brunch with the papers till midnight with a glass of wine.

So traditional teak garden furniture is not enough. It needs masses of pretty cushions, which can be kept in a dry storeroom in a willow basket ready to bring out when the sun shines. The slatted teak table looks prettier for dinner if given an antique tablecloth under a fine array of glasses, silver and sharply folded napkins. You can change the mood in a trice and make an Italian lunch of black olives, salami, cheese and bread on bright pottery casually set down on a plain bright linen cloth or one of those complex Provençal prints which at once recall the South.

Garden rooms and conservatories are prime sites for squashy cushions on cane chairs. Here are places to use pretty chintzes adorned with simple patterns of fuchsias or geraniums of the type for which Colefax and Fowler are famous, or an evocative modern floral of rosebuds and carnations – sweetly old-fashioned designs imperceptibly modernized by a change of colour and scale. If the garden room is by the sea, use stripes and ticking, blues and whites; if you find a nice warm day for the garden room in Scotland, add lashings of tartan and tweed to the chairs.

LEFT It's not only the bottle of wine that makes this outdoor picnic in an olive grove inviting. The strung and striped hammock and oversized cushion are both in bright colours, competing with the Mediterranean light.
BELOW Cheaper, plain tablecloths can be tweaked to suit a decorating scheme by sewing on ribbons. Here, the choice is a plain cotton one and a fancier ombre style with picot edging. Note how the ribbons reappear on the vase of flowers.
OPPOSITE PAGE A slung wooden hammock gives character to the verandah of an East Hampton guest house. Its cotton cushions, in old striped and floral fabrics, match the dark green paint of the woodwork.

Small outdoor spaces in the centre of cities offer the opportunity for a touch of *rus in urbe*. If you have only a basement, give it a single bamboo, a tiny dribbling fountain and a concrete shelf to act as a seat, with one thick, white cushion on the seat and another at the back. Keep all the colours cool, for it is in the centre of the city where you need most calm. Alternatively, imitate the quiet courtyards of Moorish Spain or Florentine palazzi by adding comfortable piles of cushions to built-in seats or iron chairs grouped around an ornamental fountain and hanging baskets of grèen ferns and exotic leaves.

Even in midwinter, when a well-heated garden room beckons on a rare sunny day, the atmosphere should be summery. Keep the colour scheme simple, ideally reflecting the planting of the garden beyond. Green and white are obvious choices; you could add gentian blue and a citrus yellow to give the impression of ultramarine and white bluebells and Welsh poppies growing among the ivies outside; or stick to a couple of shades of bright red to startle among the green – but never be tempted to go for a riot of colour in fabrics. The result will be as messy as a riot of colour in the border.

For shade in the real outdoors, choose plants carefully grown over netting or big white canvas umbrellas imported from Italy (and you could buy an overhead mobile gas heater to take advantage of fine spring and autumn days). Any blinds used to shade the glass roof in a conservatory or garden room should be practical and unobtrusive – wooden slats, pinoleum or plain, natural canvas – because it is preferable to avoid drawing attention to the roof at the expense of the comfortable furnishings below.

FABRIC CARE

I've written in earlier parts of the book about choosing the right fabric for the job – and it is crucial. Unless you are devoted to shabby chic, all soft furnishings should be meticulously clean. Modern fabrics make this simple: if they can't be laundered, they can be dry-cleaned, with the caveat that it is simpler to dry-clean large volumes of washable fabrics than to wash them. Otherwise the washer may explode, the fabric come out only patchily clean, and the ironing fail to remove all the wrinkles.

When you buy any new fabric, ask how it can be cleaned. Make sure that any accessories you add – tassels, braiding, borders – will react in the same way. You don't want to have to unpick bits before the whole is cleaned. Ask, too, about whether cottons for loose covers, curtains and valances are likely to shrink – even if the answer is no, have them laundered before they are made up. Find out about colour fastness and reaction to strong sunlight. For tailored upholstery, call in specialist dry-cleaners to work in your home.

Some antique fabrics are as easy to care for as modern fabrics: old linen towels, sheets and monochrome hangings can cope with a session in the washing machine. Other textiles, such as paisley shawls, antique toiles and heavy wool curtains, can be carefully dry-cleaned. Materials such as wool embroideries, lace and heavy silks can be washed by hand at a cool temperature in pure soapflakes. I know that some antiques dealers put their patchwork quilts into washing machines on a cool cycle but I have never dared to do so myself. If you are buying such an item from a dealer, ask at the time about how to care for it – but take any advice with a pinch of salt, on the grounds that the dealer is trying to make a sale. Most cottons can be washed in a machine, but the colours should be checked in advance for fastness. Do a dummy run, if you can. It's preferable to treat a quilt as an ornament and take it off before going to bed.

There are trained conservators who will repair any antique fabric for you – at enormous cost and delays. If you want to make a repair yourself, always use the same fibre for the sewing thread as in the fabric: silk with silk, wool with wool, cotton with cotton.

Keep wools in storage with mothballs near but not touching them. Fine textiles should be wrapped in acid-free tissue paper and given some ventilation to keep them free from mould. Inspect them regularly and change how they are folded. It may seem like a lot of effort, but it's worth it.

RIGHT A small gingham checked cotton has been used for this quickly made kitchen blind. The blind's position means that the fabric should be easy to remove and wash.
FAR RIGHT A large gingham check is perfectly at ease in this formal living room. Added clout has been given by the bobble trim and fabric ties to poles, which must be as easily cleaned as the curtains.
OPPOSITE PAGE If you can find two fabrics that are a close – but not exact – match, use them for upholstery and curtaining. But such pale shades are a bad idea if upholstery is in daily use.

PRACTICALITIES

equipment and techniques

The projects on the following pages – which range from simple curtains to a fitted chair cover – vary in the level of experience required, but most of the techniques involved in making them will be familiar from dressmaking. The equipment needed is minimal but, to help you to achieve lasting and professional results, it is worth investing in the best possible tools and materials.

BASIC SEWING KIT

Sewing machine

Modern electronic sewing machines have many advanced stitching features – but most soft furnishings require only a basic straight stitch and a zigzag for neatening seams. Always use a sharp needle and match its thickness to the weight of the fabric. The finest needles have the lowest numbers – so use size 8 for sheer curtains, 12 for most projects and a size 16 for heavy canvas.

Scissors

A range of scissors is essential for anyone who is serious about making cushions, curtains and other soft furnishings. Each pair should be kept for its own purpose:

Dressmaking shears with long blades are used for cutting out and should be kept well sharpened. The handles are bent at an angle so that they can cut accurately.

Sewing scissors are smaller and have straight handles. Use these for trimming seams and clipping corners.

Embroidery scissors have short, pointed blades, which makes them ideal for trimming thread and notching seam allowances.

Paper scissors should be kept specially for cutting out patterns and templates.

Iron

Hems and seams must be pressed well, so you need a good steam iron and a large ironing board. Use a cleaning cloth to remove any build-up and descale the iron regularly. A dressmaker's sleeve board is useful for detailed work.

Needles

Hand-sewing needles come in various sizes for different tasks. Medium-length sharps are best for general sewing and tacking, and shorter betweens can be used for slip stitch. Crewel needles have an extra long eye designed for embroidery threads.

Thimble

A flat-top metal thimble should be used to protect the fingers when tacking heavy fabrics together but it may take a while to get used to.

Dressmaker's pins

These can be used for fine fabrics; larger glass-headed pins show up better on thicker material. Check that they are made from rustless steel.

Sewing thread

Always choose a thread made from the same weight and fibre as the fabric being stitched. Mercerized cotton has a smooth surface and should be used for stitching cotton and linens.

Polyester thread is finer and can be used for mixed fabrics. Match the colour as closely as possible, and choose a darker shade if an exact match is not possible.

Tacking thread

The loosely spun thread used for tacking is not mercerized, which means it breaks easily and can be unpicked without damaging a finished seam. Use a contrasting colour that shows up well when tacking stitches are being removed.

Marking tools

Tailor's chalk, which comes in a thin, solid block, produces a fine line that brushes away easily. Use white for dark fabrics and the coloured versions to mark paler cloth.

Chalk pencils can be sharpened to a fine point for detailed marking.

Dressmaker's pens have a water-soluble or light-sensitive ink that washes out or fades completely a few hours after use without leaving any marks.

Measurements

Precise measurement is vital, so obtain a good tape measure that will not stretch with use and become inaccurate. Conversions are not exact. **Always follow either the metric or the imperial measurements** when making up a project.

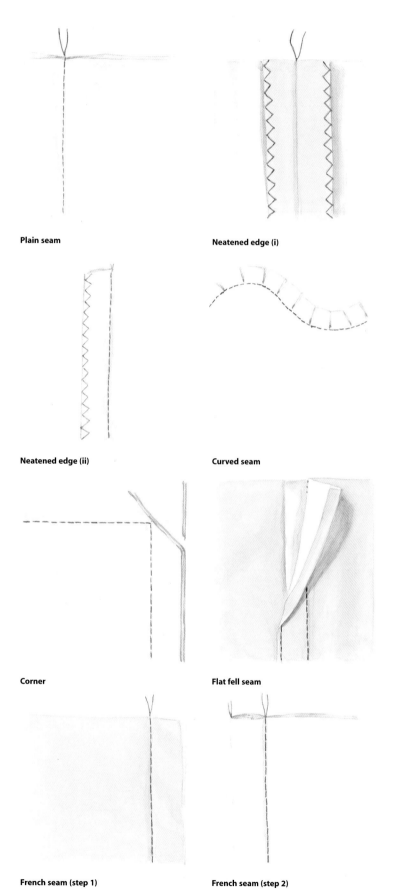

Plain seam

Neatened edge (i)

Neatened edge (ii)

Curved seam

Corner

Flat fell seam

French seam (step 1)

French seam (step 2)

SEAMS

The extra fabric needed to join two pieces of fabric is given as the seam allowance. To keep it consistent, match the raw edges to the corresponding line on the bed of the sewing machine when stitching.

Plain seam Line up the two raw edges with right sides facing. Pin together at 5–10cm (2–4in) intervals, inserting the pins at right angles to the fabric or parallel to the edge. Tack, then machine stitch along the seam line. Press the seam open or to one side as directed and unpick the tacking.

Neatened edge The cut edge of a plain seam may fray, especially if an item is washed. To prevent this, a line of zigzag or overlock stitch can be worked along each raw edge before seaming if the seam is to be pressed open (i). If the seam is to be pressed to one side, the seam allowance can be trimmed and the two edges joined together with a zigzag (ii).

Curved seam The allowance on a curved seam has to be trimmed back to 1cm ($\frac{1}{3}$in) and clipped so that the seam will lie flat. For an outside curve, make small notches; on an inside curve, snip a short distance into the seam allowance at regular intervals.

Corner To sew round a right-angled corner, stitch to the end of the seam allowance. Lift the presser foot, leaving the needle down. Turn the fabric through 90 degrees, and continue stitching. Clip off the corner to within 2mm ($\frac{1}{16}$in) of the stitching before turning through, so that it will lie flat.

Flat fell seam This seam shows on the right side as two parallel rows of stitches. With wrong sides facing, make a plain seam as above, then trim one seam allowance to 6mm ($\frac{1}{4}$in). Press under 3mm ($\frac{1}{8}$in) along the other allowance and tack the fold to the main fabric over the shortened edge. Machine stitch close to fold.

French seam Used for joining lightweight or sheer fabrics, this seam encloses the raw edges on the wrong side. With wrong sides facing, seam the fabric 8mm ($\frac{3}{8}$in) from the edge. Trim the allowance to 6mm ($\frac{1}{4}$in) and fold the right sides together. Stitch again, 8mm ($\frac{3}{8}$in) from the edge.

HEMS

The finish to the lower edge of a piece of fabric depends on its weight:

Single hem Used for heavier linens and furnishing fabrics. Zigzag the raw edge and press the turning up to the required length on the wrong side. Pin and tack, then sew in place by hand or machine stitch just below the zigzag.

Double hem Consists of one narrow and one deeper turning or two equal turnings, which give a firmer edge to finer fabrics. Press under 6mm (¼in) along the raw edge, then turn up to length as directed. Pin and tack, then either machine stitch close to the inner fold or finish by hand. A machine stitch is used for chair covers, but curtain hems are hand finished for a better result.

MITRES

When two hems meet at right angles, the surplus fabric should be neatened with a mitre to avoid a bulky corner.

Single hem Press under the turnings along each edge, then unfold them. Fold the corner inwards at a right angle so that the creases line up to make a square. Refold the hems, then slip stitch the folded edges together.

Double hem For two double hems of equal depth, press under both turnings. Unfold the second fold only, then turn in the corner, refold and stitch as above. If one hem is deeper than the other, follow the method for an angled mitre described on pages 158–59.

HAND STITCHING

All the projects in this section are stitched by machine, but hand sewing is vital for tacking and finishing off hems, mitres and some seams.

Slip stitch Used to join two folded edges or to secure a folded hem. Bring the needle out through the fold and pick up two threads of the other fabric. Pass the needle back through the fold for 6mm (¼in) and repeat to the end.

Herringbone stitch Creates a flat, unobtrusive hem for curtains. Bring the needle up inside the hem and make a diagonal stitch up to the right, then a short horizontal stitch to the left. Work a diagonal stitch down to the right and, taking the needle through the top layer of the hem, make a short horizontal stitch to the left. Repeat these two stitches to continue.

Stab stitch A firm stitch used to secure two or more layers of fabric. Bring the needle up through all the layers, then take it back down 2mm (¹⁄₁₆in) away.

Buttonhole stitch Mark a line the length of your button and outline it with running stitch. Cut along the line and anchor the thread on the wrong side. Insert the needle at the top left corner and bring it out through the opening. Loop the thread under the point and pull through. Repeat to the end and along the lower edge.

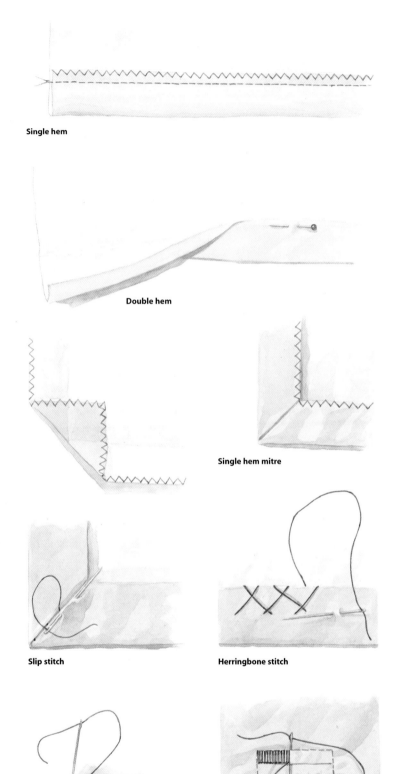

Single hem

Double hem

Single hem mitre

Slip stitch

Herringbone stitch

Stab stitch

Buttonhole stitch

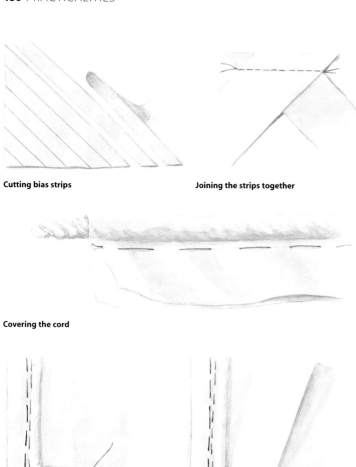

Cutting bias strips

Joining the strips together

Covering the cord

Piping round a corner

Pinning second piece of fabric

Piping on a curve

Making a join in a round of piping

PIPING

Piping is a soft cotton cord covered with a narrow strip of fabric. It is sewn into a seam to make the seam more hard-wearing and to add a decorative line to a cushion cover or a loose cover that emphasizes the shape of the cover. If it is not labelled as 'pre-shrunk', the cord should be washed at a high temperature before it is sewn into the seam. Piping cord is available in several thicknesses: the most commonly used is size 4, which requires a 4cm (1½ in) wide strip of fabric.

Covering the cord

Make a bias strip the same length as the cord. Mark a diagonal line on the fabric at 45 degrees to the edge. Draw a series of lines parallel to this, 4cm (1½ in) apart, and cut along them. With right sides facing, sew the strips together at right angles 1cm (½ in) from the edge. Press the seams open. With the right side outwards, fold the strip around the cord and pin then tack in place 3mm (⅛ in) from the cord.

Piping a seam

Pin then tack the piping to the right side of the fabric, lining up the raw edges. Cut 6mm (¼ in) notches into the seam allowance on both the bias strip and the main fabric to give a smooth line on a curved seam – or clip into the seam allowance on the bias strip at a corner. With right sides facing, pin the second piece of fabric in place. Tack, then machine stitch, using a zip foot to sew close to the cord. Unpick the tacking.

Making a join in a round of piping

A join in a continuous length of piping, or in a round of piping, can be made inconspicuous by positioning it next to a seam line.

Tack the piping in place, leaving a 2.5cm (1in) overlap on each side of the join. Unpick the tacking for 3cm (1¼ in) at each loose end. Trim the cord so that the ends butt and stitch them together loosely. Tack under the end of one bias strip so that it lines up with the seam. Fold it over the other strip and tack both ends in place. Machine stitch as close to the cord as possible, using a zip foot.

ZIPS

Zips are available with either metal or plastic teeth, and come in a range of lengths and colours. To insert a zip in a flat seam, pin and tack the two sides together along the seam allowance, then machine stitch each end, leaving a central gap 1.5cm (½ in) longer than the zip. Reinforce both ends of the stitching. Press the seam open. Close the zip, then tack it in place on the wrong side of the opening. Stitch the zip in place from the right side, using the zip foot to sew 3mm (⅛ in) from the teeth.

MACHINE APPLIQUÉ

Appliquéd motifs on soft furnishings may need to be dry-cleaned or laundered, so they should be hard-wearing. A lasting finish can be created by joining them to the background fabric with iron-on bonding web and finishing the raw edges with machine stitch.

Draw the motif to full size, reversing the outline if it is not symmetrical, and trace it through onto the paper side of the bonding web. Cut the shape out roughly and place it, adhesive side down, onto the wrong side of the appliqué fabric. Iron in place following the manufacturer's instructions. Cut out carefully around the pencil outline, then peel away the backing paper. Position the motif on the background fabric, adhesive side down, and iron in place as directed.

Thread the machine with sewing cotton to match the appliqué and adjust to a medium-width satin stitch. Working steadily, sew around the motif so that the stitches cover the raw edge completely. Decrease the width of the stitch as you approach a corner or point to create a neat, tapered finish.

Iron-on stencil

Machine satin stitch

MEASURING UP A WINDOW FOR CURTAINS

The curtain fitting – rod, pole or track – should be in place before you start.

Width (A) Measure from the centre of the window to the end of the pole. If the fitting is made in two parts, add on extra for the overlap. Some fittings have an angled return at each corner to accommodate the fabric when the curtains are drawn back; add on this length if necessary.

Length (B) Measure from the top edge of the track or the loops on the rings to the floor – or, for a shorter curtain, measure to just below the sill.

PATTERNED CURTAIN FABRICS

Matching repeats

Patterned fabrics have to be matched up across both curtains to make a pair and also when two lengths are joined together to make a wide curtain. Measure the depth of the pattern repeat and add this onto each length when calculating the fabric required. When cutting out, ensure that each piece starts at the same point on the design.

Joining fabric widths

Patterned fabrics should be joined so that the design matches horizontally across the seam. Press under the seam allowance on one side and pin the fold to the second length so that the patterns line up. Tack together with a long slip stitch. Fold right sides together and machine stitch along the tacked line. Neaten the raw edges. A centre seam can look clumsy. It can be avoided by cutting the second length of fabric into two panels and sewing one panel to each side of the first length.

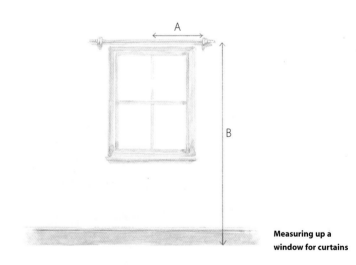

Measuring up a window for curtains

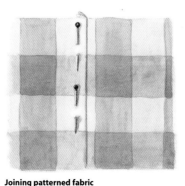

Joining patterned fabric

Joining fabric widths

unlined curtains

Unlined, café-style curtains are usually made from a lighter weight fabric than lined curtains, which allows daylight to filter through. Ready-made tapes designed to create instant pleated headings are easy to use – but it is worth making headings by hand, in the traditional way, because they give a crisper, more professional finish and can be adapted to create accurate pleats on striped or checked fabrics. Buckram – coarse cloth stiffened with size – gives rigidity to the headings.

Materials and equipment

lightweight to midweight fabric
matching sewing thread
dressmaker's pins
heading buckram 10cm (4in) deep
basic sewing kit
tailor's chalk
curtain hooks

Measuring up and cutting out

The finished size of each curtain depends on the shape of the window and the type of curtain rail or pole used. (For advice on measuring up a window, see page 157.) The final width = A; the final length = B.

Calculating the pleat allowance

The pleats are 12cm (5in) apart, and there should be as many pleats as gaps between them, including one half-gap at each end. To find out the number of pleats, divide A by 12cm (5in) and round up or down to the nearest whole number. Multiply this figure by 15cm (6in) to find out how much extra fabric is needed to make the pleats.

Curtain panel

If necessary, join one or more fabric widths to make the panel the correct size. (For advice on joining fabric widths, see page 157.)

width = A *plus* pleat allowance *plus* 12cm (4in) hem allowance *plus* overlap and reveal allowances if required
depth = B *plus* 11cm (4½in) heading allowance *plus* 16cm (6in) hem allowance

Buckram

length = 2cm (1in) shorter than width of curtain panel

Working out the total length of fabric required

Divide the width of the curtain panel by the width of the chosen fabric and round up to the nearest whole number. Multiply by the depth of the curtain panel, then by the number of curtains required. Allow an extra 3cm (1in) for each metre (yard) of non-preshrunk fabric. Remember to add any extra fabric needed to match up the repeats on a patterned fabric (see page 157).

1 For each curtain, turn under and press a 3cm (1in) double hem along each side edge and a 8cm (3in) double hem along the bottom edge.

2 Mark three points with pins: the corner, the inside edge of the side turning where it meets the hem, and the corresponding point on the hem.

3 Unfold all the creases, then refold one turning along each edge. Fold the corner inwards so that all three pins line up.

4 Press lightly, then refold and pin down the second turnings. Slip stitch the two sides of the mitre together, from the corner inwards.

5 Pin and tack the side and bottom hems. Machine or slip stitch the side hems, and slip or herringbone stitch the bottom hem.

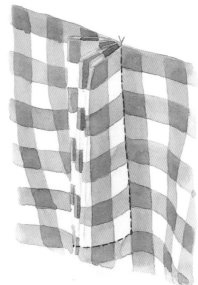

10 Hand pleat the fabric into three equal-sized small folds, then press them into position. Pin, tack and machine stitch across the folds 1cm ($\frac{1}{2}$ in) below the bottom edge of the buckram, at right angles to the pleat lines.

11 Sew a curtain hook securely to the top of each pleat, on the wrong side of the heading. If the curtain is to hang from decorative rings on a pole, the top of the hooks should be 1cm ($\frac{1}{2}$ in) below the top edge of the curtain. If the curtain is to hang from a track, the top of the hooks should be positioned 5cm (2in) down, so that the track is concealed when the curtains are drawn.

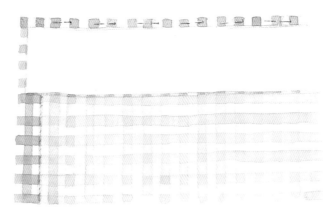

7 Slip stitch together the side edges of the fold.

8 Using tailor's chalk, mark the positions of the pleats and the gaps between them along the wrong side of the top edge.

9 Pin two pleat lines together to make a large pleat. Tack and machine stitch on the right side to just below the bottom edge of the buckram.

6 Press under a 1cm ($\frac{1}{2}$ in) turning along the top raw edge. Starting 1cm ($\frac{1}{2}$ in) in from one corner, pin the top edge of the buckram under the fold. Tack and machine stitch it in place. Fold the buckram to the wrong side and press along the fold.

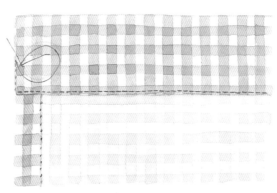

cupboard curtains

A minimal amount of sewing is needed to create these curtains. Each panel is a simple rectangle, hemmed along each side and gathered at the top and bottom. The gingham curtains are drawn up with elastic and pinned in place, while the more formal folds of the plain curtains are created by using sprung curtain wire. Washable lightweight and sheer cotton furnishing or dressmaking fabrics are most suitable because they hang in fine folds. Small prints, plain colours or geometric stripes and checks work best; large-scale patterns become lost when gathered.

Materials and equipment

basic sewing kit
cotton fabric
matching sewing thread

for the gingham curtains

narrow braid elastic
small safety pin
drawing pins

for the plain curtains

sprung curtain wire
heavy wire cutters
four screw-eyes and
four cup hooks for each curtain
bradawl

Measuring up and cutting out
The finished curtain should overlap the glass or mesh by 3cm (1in) at each side.

width = $1\frac{1}{2}$ to 2 times the width of door panel (depending on weight of fabric) *plus* 6cm ($2\frac{1}{2}$ in) overlap *plus* 4cm ($1\frac{1}{2}$ in) hem allowance

length = depth of panel *plus* 6cm (2in) overlap *plus* 4cm ($1\frac{1}{2}$ in) clearance *plus* 6cm ($2\frac{1}{2}$ in) for the cased headings

Making the curtains

1 Iron the fabric to remove any creases. Press under 1cm ($\frac{1}{2}$ in) along each long edge. Press under another 1cm ($\frac{1}{2}$ in) to make a double hem, then pin, tack and machine stitch close to the inner fold. If the fabric is not the same on both sides, make the hems on the right side of the curtain.

2 Press under 1cm ($\frac{1}{2}$ in) along the bottom edge, then press under another 2cm ($\frac{3}{4}$ in). Pin, tack and machine stitch close to the inner fold to form a narrow channel or cased heading. Do the same at the top edge and finish off any loose threads.

Hanging the gingham curtains

1 Cut a length of braid elastic 4cm (1½in) shorter than the width of the door panel. Fix a safety pin to one end and pass it along the bottom casing. Draw the elastic through until the loose end is in line with the opening, then stab stitch it securely in place, through the front and back of the casing.

2 Bring the pin out at the other opening and sew the end of the elastic to the casing. Thread the top casing in the same way.

3 With hems and casings facing the door, attach the curtain to the inside of the cupboard using three drawing pins at top edge and three at the bottom.

Hanging the plain curtains

1 Mark four points on the back of the cupboard door, 3cm (1in) from each corner of the opening. Use a bradawl to make a hole at each mark and screw the hooks into the door so that they face upwards.

2 Twist a screw-eye into one end of the sprung wire and loop it over a hook. Stretch the wire across to the second hook – it should be taut but not too tight – and make a pencil mark on the wire where they meet.

3 Cut the wire to length and twist the second eye in place. Do the same with the second piece of wire.

4 Feed the two wires into the top and bottom casings; the fabric will gather up as it goes through.

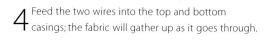

5 Hook the top wire in place so that the hems and casings face the door, then slip the bottom screw-eyes over the hooks.

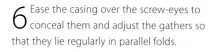

6 Ease the casing over the screw-eyes to conceal them and adjust the gathers so that they lie regularly in parallel folds.

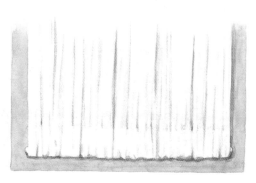

Roman blind

This type of Roman blind is made from a lined rectangular panel, weighted by a lath, with cords on the reverse side. It is hung from a batten, which can be fixed in a window recess or mounted on a wall. A closely woven cotton fabric such as ticking is easy to sew and will endure heavy use.

Materials and equipment

ticking or similar striped fabric

white lining fabric

1.5cm (^{1}/$_2$in) plastic rings

matching sewing thread

nylon blind cord

blind acorn

basic sewing kit

dressmaker's pins

long ruler

tailor's chalk

wooden lath, 2cm (^{3}/$_4$in) shorter than finished width of blind

3 small screw-eyes

3cm x 3cm (1^1/$_4$ x 1^1/$_4$in) wooden batten, 5mm (^{1}/$_4$in) shorter than finished width of blind

staple gun

small safety pin

two small angle brackets, screws and rawlplugs or four long screws and rawlplugs

cleat and screws

drill

screwdriver

If the blind is to be mounted on the wall, the ends and underside of the batten will be visible, so the wood should be painted to match the colour of the blind.

Measuring up

If blind is to hang in a window recess
width (A) = width of recess *minus* 2cm (^{3}/$_4$in)
length (B) = from top of recess to sill

If blind is to hang outside a window recess or over a frame
width (A) = width of frame or recess *plus* 6cm (2^1/$_2$in)
length (B) = from top of batten to 3cm (1in) below bottom edge of frame or sill

Cutting out

Blind and lining alike
width = A *plus* 4cm (1^1/$_2$in)
depth= B *plus* 12cm (5in)

Three cords cut to the following lengths: 2B, 2B *plus* ^{1}/$_4$A, 2B *plus* A

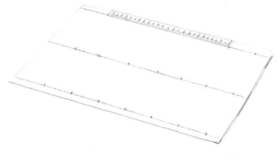

1 Mark a chalk line down the centre of the right side of the lining, then draw two more lines 5cm (2in) in from each long edge. Starting 15cm (6in) up from the bottom edge, mark a series of 30cm (12in) intervals along each line. Leave a space of at least 20cm (8in) at the top edge to accommodate the blind when it is drawn up.

2 Hand stitch a small plastic ring securely to each of the marks, then brush away the chalk lines.

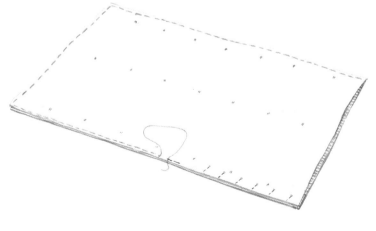

3 With right sides facing, pin together the long side edges and top edge of the blind and the lining. Tack, then machine stitch, leaving a seam allowance of 2cm (^{3}/$_4$in). Clip the corners, turn right side out and press.

4 Make a casing to hold the lath at the bottom of the blind on the same side as the tapes. Press under a 2cm ($\frac{3}{4}$in) turning along the raw edge, then press under a further 4cm ($1\frac{1}{4}$in) turning. Tack down, then machine stitch, 3mm ($\frac{1}{8}$in) from the inside fold.

5 Slip the lath inside the casing and secure the open ends with slip stitch.

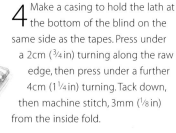

6 If the blind is to fit in a recess, drill four equally spaced holes through the batten from top to bottom. Mark the centre back of the batten. Then fix the screw-eyes to the underside so that one lies at the top of each line of rings.

7 Press a 2cm ($\frac{3}{4}$in) turning to the wrong side along the blind's top edge. With the right side of the blind facing down, staple the centre top of the blind to the centre back of the batten, so that the fold lies along the back edge of the batten. Continue stapling towards each end: the fabric will overlap the batten slightly.

8 With the blind laid out flat and the rings uppermost, thread the cords in order from the shortest to the longest. Fasten a small safety pin to one end of the first cord. Thread the cord through the first screw-eye on the left, then down through the first line of rings. Undo the pin and sew the end of the cord securely to the final ring. (For a blind that pulls up from the left, start with the first screw-eye on the right.)

9 Thread the second cord through the first and centre screw-eyes, then through the centre line of rings. Attach the third cord in the same way, passing it through the preceding screw-eyes. Thread all the loose ends through the acorn and adjust them so that they are the same length. Knot securely, trim and slide the acorn over the knot.

10 A wall-mounted blind is fixed on or above the window frame, using a small-angle bracket at each end of the batten. If the blind is to fit in a window recess, drill three holes into the top of the recess, in line with the holes in the batten, and use long screws and rawlplugs to fix the batten in place. Screw a cleat on or near the frame, on the same side as the cords.

linen bedspread

This lightweight summer bedcover is made from strips of toning linen which have been joined together with durable French seams and bound at the top and bottom edges with a contrasting dark fabric. The measurements given can be adapted to fit a bed of any width.

Materials and equipment

pale-coloured linen

white linen

dark-coloured linen

matching sewing thread

dressmaker's pins

sewing machine

sewing kit

Measuring up

width (A) = width of bed *plus* 2 x height

length (B) = length of bed *plus* height

Cutting out

Panel of coloured linen
(cut three)
width = 4C *plus* 3cm (1in)
seam allowance
length = B

Panel of white linen (cut two)
width = C *plus* 3cm (1in)
seam allowance
length = B

Binding (cut two)
width = 12cm (5in)
length = A *plus* 10cm (4in)

Panel widths Divide the finished width A by 14 to find width C, the width of the white panels. The coloured panels are four times wider (4C) than the white panels.

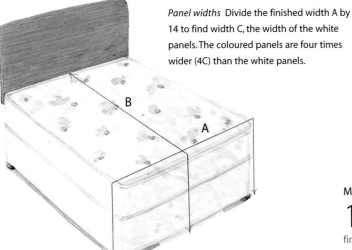

Making up the bedspread

1 With wrong sides facing, pin and tack one long edge of the first white panel to one long edge of the first coloured panel.

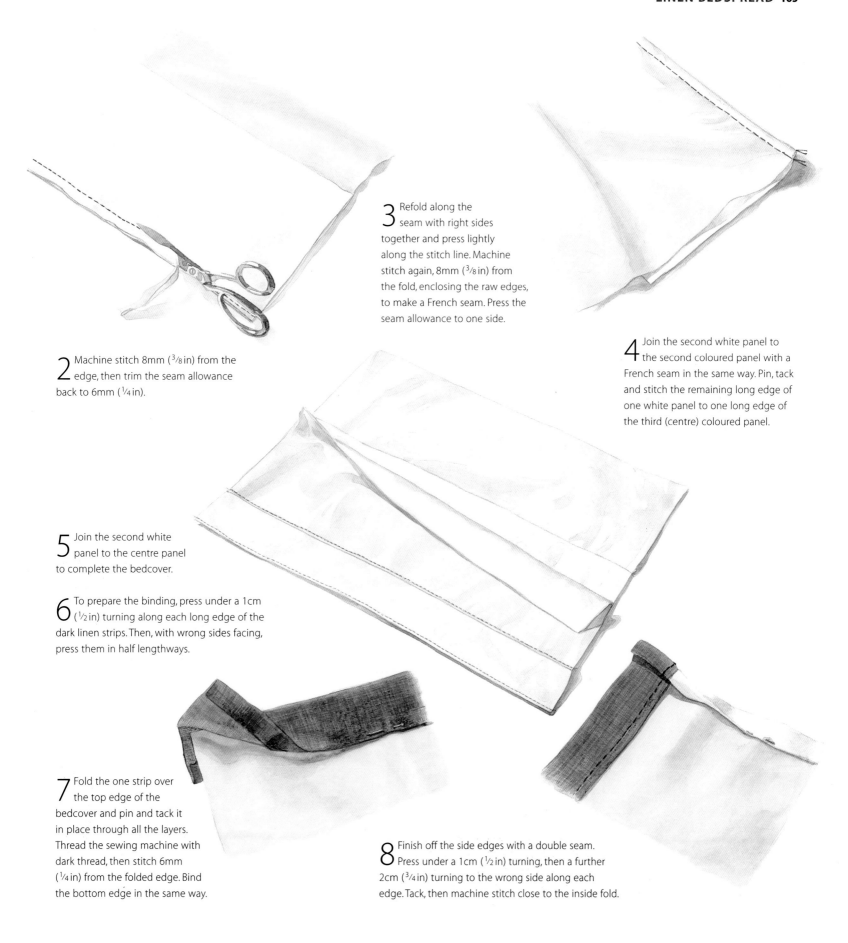

3 Refold along the seam with right sides together and press lightly along the stitch line. Machine stitch again, 8mm (³⁄₈ in) from the fold, enclosing the raw edges, to make a French seam. Press the seam allowance to one side.

2 Machine stitch 8mm (³⁄₈ in) from the edge, then trim the seam allowance back to 6mm (¼ in).

4 Join the second white panel to the second coloured panel with a French seam in the same way. Pin, tack and stitch the remaining long edge of one white panel to one long edge of the third (centre) coloured panel.

5 Join the second white panel to the centre panel to complete the bedcover.

6 To prepare the binding, press under a 1cm (½ in) turning along each long edge of the dark linen strips. Then, with wrong sides facing, press them in half lengthways.

7 Fold the one strip over the top edge of the bedcover and pin and tack it in place through all the layers. Thread the sewing machine with dark thread, then stitch 6mm (¼ in) from the folded edge. Bind the bottom edge in the same way.

8 Finish off the side edges with a double seam. Press under a 1cm (½ in) turning, then a further 2cm (¾ in) turning to the wrong side along each edge. Tack, then machine stitch close to the inside fold.

chair back and tie-on seat cover

This informal Scandinavian-style chair back and seat cover, which match the soft furnishings used on the bed, have practical origins. Similar two-part covers were first used to protect expensively upholstered furniture from dust or bright sunlight, but they eventually became fashionable in their own right. All padded chairs vary in shape and are often contoured, so the seat template has to be modelled directly over the chair. Take time doing this to ensure that you achieve a perfect fit.

Materials and equipment

150cm (60in) gingham furnishing fabric 150cm (60in) wide

140cm (56in) cotton tape for ties

basic sewing kit

matching sewing thread

pencil and dressmaker's squared paper

dressmaker's pins

Measuring up and cutting out

Chair back (cut two)

width = top edge measured from centre of outside edges of struts (A) *plus* 2cm (³/₄in) *plus* 3cm (1in) seam allowance

depth = from centre of top of strut to 2cm (³/₄in) from seat (B) *plus* 4cm (1¹/₂in) seam and hem allowance

E = depth of cushioned part

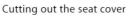

Cutting out the seat cover

1 Measure the width (C *plus* 2E) and depth (D *plus* 2E). Cut the paper to this size and pin it to the seat. Fold and pin a dart at each front corner.

2 Use a pencil to mark on the paper the inside points of the back struts. Cut diagonally from the back corners to these points, then cut out shapes to fit around the base of each strut.

3 Pin the side drops to the seat and trim so that they line up with the back corners of the chair legs. Mark the bottom edge of the seat with a pencil line. Unpin the pattern.

4 Cut around the pencil outline and along the folds at the front corners. Fold the template in half widthways to check that it is symmetrical. Pin it to the fabric, following the grain.

5 Cut out, adding a seam allowance of 1.5cm (¹/₂in) at each corner and a 3cm (1in) hem along each drop.

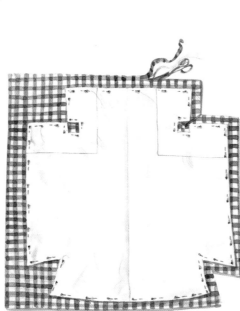

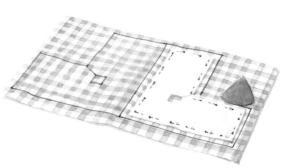

6 The back corners are reinforced with facings in the same fabric. To make the pattern, draw a line 8cm (3in) from one corner of the seat template and cut out. Cut two pieces, allowing an extra 1.5cm (¹/₂in) all round.

Making up the seat cover

1 Cut the tape into four 35cm (14in) lengths. Tack in place on the back and side drops 2cm (³⁄₄in) away from the corners.

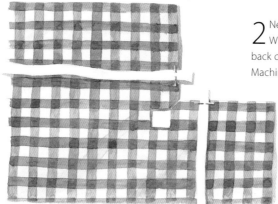

2 Neaten the two long straight edges of each facing. With right sides together, pin the facings to the back corners of the seat cover, enclosing the tapes. Machine stitch 1.5cm (¹⁄₂in) from the inside edge.

3 Clip the seam allowance at the inside corners and trim the outside corners. Turn the facings through and top stitch the seam.

4 Neaten the edges of the front and side drops. With right sides facing, pin and tack together and machine stitch 1.5cm (¹⁄₂in) from the edge. Press the seams open and turn right sides out.

5 Press under a 1.5 cm (¹⁄₂in) double hem around the outside edge, and pin and tack in place. Tie the cover in place, check that the hem is level and machine stitch close to the inside fold. Press the cover.

Making up the chair back

1 Neaten the top and side edges of each rectangle. With right sides facing, pin and tack the neatened edges together, then machine stitch, leaving a seam allowance of 1.5cm (¹⁄₂in).

2 Slip the cover over the chair. Fold the top and side seams together at one top corner to form a triangle, then pin them together along the edge of the chair back. Stitch along this line, then trim the seam allowance to 8mm (³⁄₈in) and neaten. Dart the other corner in the same way and press the seams open.

3 Press a 1.5cm (¹⁄₂in) double hem around the lower edge, then tack and machine stitch down. Turn right sides out and press.

slip cover for a dining chair

This cover is constructed from a series of rectangles to give a close, tailored fit. The contrasting border and appliquéd motif add elegant finishing touches. Box pleats at each corner accommodate the splay of the legs, and no additional fastenings are required. This design is suitable for a simple upright chair with a narrow metal or wooden frame without any upholstery or carving. The back should be no deeper than 3cm (1¼ in).

Materials and equipment

2.5m (2¾ yds) plain furnishing fabric 150cm (60in) wide

50cm (20in) contrast fabric 150cm (60in) wide

3m (3¼ yds) medium piping cord

basic sewing kit

squared pattern paper

dressmaker's pins

matching sewing thread

tailor's chalk

Measuring up

Take each measurement from the widest point of the chair.

Inside back

top width = top edge from centre of side struts (A)

bottom width = back edge from centre of side struts (C)

depth = from centre top of side strut to seat (B)

Seat

back width = back edge from centre of side struts (C)

front width = front edge from corner to corner (D)

depth = side edge from front corner to centre of back strut (E)

Outside back

top width = top edge from centre of side struts (A)

centre and bottom widths = back edge from centre of side struts (C)

plus 2 pleats (16cm/6in)

depth of back = from centre top of side strut to seat (B)

depth of skirt = from top edge of seat to floor (F) *minus* border (10cm/4in)

Back border

width = as bottom width of outside back

depth = 12cm (5in)

Front skirt

width = front edge of seat from corner to corner (D)

plus 2 pleats (16cm/6in)

depth = from top edge of seat to floor (F) *minus* border (10cm/4in)

Front border

width = as front skirt

depth = 12cm (5in)

Side skirt

width = side edge of seat from front corner to centre of back strut (E)

plus 6 pleats (48cm/18in)

depth = from top edge of seat to floor *minus* border (10cm/4in)

Side border

width = as side skirt

depth = 12cm (5in)

Piping

length = A + 2B + 2E + D (to fit around perimeter of the back and seat)

plus 5cm (2in) to make the join

For guidance on how to make the piping, see page 156.

Making the pattern and cutting out

1 Make a copy of the pattern diagram and fill in the measurements.

2 Draw up the eight pieces to full size on squared paper and add a seam allowance of 1cm (½in) around each shape.

3 Transfer the markings: the dotted lines indicate folds and the grey arrows show the direction of the fabric grain.

4 Mark a notch at the top of each fold line where shown by the small triangles on the diagram. Leave 8cm (3in) between one notch and the next (*a* to *f*).

5 Cut out the pieces and pin them around the chair to check their accuracy; make any necessary adjustments.

6 Lay the pattern pieces out on the fabric. Check that they all follow the grain of the fabric.

7 Cut out the fabric. Then clip a 6mm (¼in) notch at the top of each pleat where shown by the small triangles. Press and label each piece.

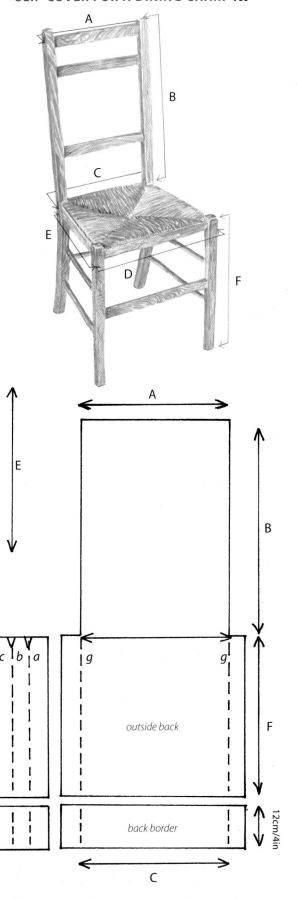

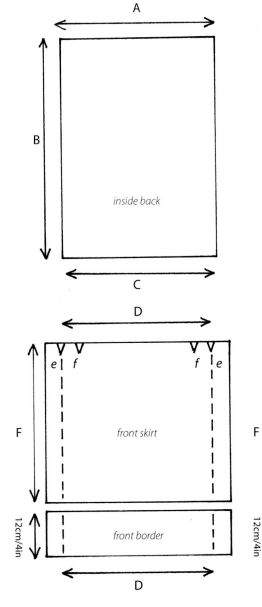

A

B

inside back

C

D

front skirt

e f   f e

front border

12cm/4in

D

C

seat

E

D

E

side skirt (cut two)

a b c d   d c b a

F

side border (cut two)

12cm/4in

D

A

B

outside back

g   g

F

back border

12cm/4in

C

Making up the cover

The seam allowance throughout is 1.5cm (½ in).

1 Neaten the top edge of the front border and the bottom edge of the front skirt. With right sides facing, pin, tack and machine stitch together the two edges, then press the seam open.

2 Sew the borders onto the bottom of the two side skirts and the outside back panel in the same way. Add any appliqué decoration to the outside back panel (see page 157).

3 With right sides facing, pin and tack one side edge of the front skirt to a side edge of one of the side skirts, taking care to match up the border seams, then machine stitch. Neaten the edges together. Press the seam allowance towards the front panel.

4 Join the other side edge of the front skirt to the other side skirt in the same way.

5 Join the other side edges of the side skirts to the side edges of the outside back panel (lower half). Neaten the seams and press towards the back panel. Turn cover right side out.

6 To make the front pleats, start at the top right corner of the front skirt. Fold along line **e**. Match notch **e** to notch **a**; line up notch **f** to the seam line and pin in place. Then match notch **c** to notch **a** and notch **d** to notch **b** and pin in place. Tack and machine stitch across the top of both folds 1.5cm (½ in) from the edge. Make the pleat at the top left corner in the same way.

7 To make the back pleats, start at the top right corner of the side skirt. Fold along line **c** (see pattern diagram, page 169). Match notch **c** to notch **a** and notch **d** to notch **b**, then pin and stitch down the fold 1.5cm (½ in) from the edge. Turn the cover wrong side out.

8 Make the second half of the pleat by folding along the seam line and matching notch **a** to point **g**. Pin, tack and machine stitch as far as the base of notch **a** 1.5cm (½ in) from the top edge. Make the other back pleat in the same way.

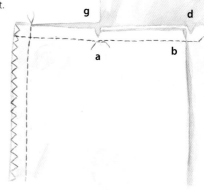

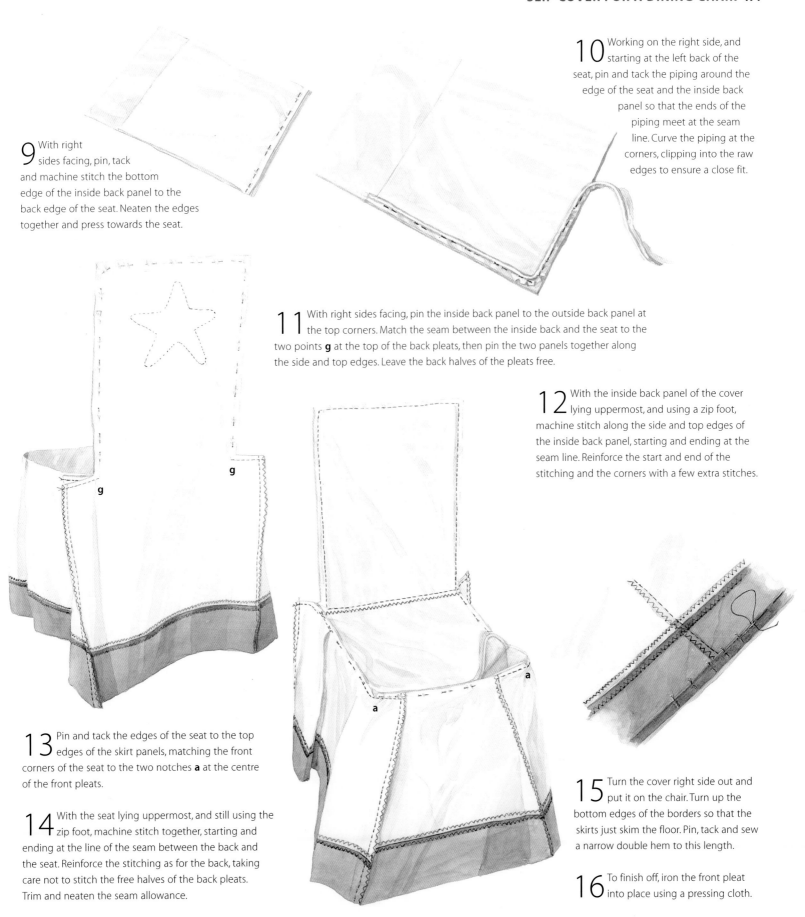

10 Working on the right side, and starting at the left back of the seat, pin and tack the piping around the edge of the seat and the inside back panel so that the ends of the piping meet at the seam line. Curve the piping at the corners, clipping into the raw edges to ensure a close fit.

9 With right sides facing, pin, tack and machine stitch the bottom edge of the inside back panel to the back edge of the seat. Neaten the edges together and press towards the seat.

11 With right sides facing, pin the inside back panel to the outside back panel at the top corners. Match the seam between the inside back and the seat to the two points **g** at the top of the back pleats, then pin the two panels together along the side and top edges. Leave the back halves of the pleats free.

12 With the inside back panel of the cover lying uppermost, and using a zip foot, machine stitch along the side and top edges of the inside back panel, starting and ending at the seam line. Reinforce the start and end of the stitching and the corners with a few extra stitches.

13 Pin and tack the edges of the seat to the top edges of the skirt panels, matching the front corners of the seat to the two notches **a** at the centre of the front pleats.

14 With the seat lying uppermost, and still using the zip foot, machine stitch together, starting and ending at the line of the seam between the back and the seat. Reinforce the stitching as for the back, taking care not to stitch the free halves of the back pleats. Trim and neaten the seam allowance.

15 Turn the cover right side out and put it on the chair. Turn up the bottom edges of the borders so that the skirts just skim the floor. Pin, tack and sew a narrow double hem to this length.

16 To finish off, iron the front pleat into place using a pressing cloth.

tie-on cushion covers

Ties made from fabric, tape or ribbon make a simple and decorative fastening for square or rectangular cushion covers. The open-ended cover looks especially effective with a contrasting cushion inside, while the pillowcase cover has a deep tuck-in flap on the inside that conceals the cushion pad and holds it in place.

Open-ended cover
Materials and equipment

main fabric
plain cushion to go inside cover
basic sewing kit
matching sewing thread
dressmaker's pins
knitting needle

Measuring up and cutting out
Front and back panels (cut two)
width = width of inner cushion (A)
plus 3cm (1in) seam allowance
depth = depth of inner cushion (B)
plus 3cm (1in) seam allowance

Facings (cut two)
width = 15cm (6in)
depth = B plus 3cm (1in)

Ties (cut four)
width = 8cm (3in)
length = 30cm (12in)

1 To make each of the four ties, fold the strip of fabric in half lengthways, with right sides facing. Machine stitch the long edge, leaving 1.5cm (½in) seam allowance, then sew across one short edge. Clip the end corners.

2 Turn each tie right side out. Ease the corners into shape using a knitting needle, and press.

3 Mark the positions of the ties on the front panel along the edge that will be the opening. Pin the ties to the right side, matching the raw edges, and tack in place. Do the same with the back panel.

4 Sew a narrow double hem along one long edge of each facing.

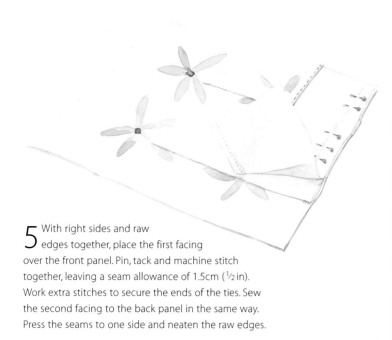

5 With right sides and raw
edges together, place the first facing
over the front panel. Pin, tack and machine stitch
together, leaving a seam allowance of 1.5cm (½in).
Work extra stitches to secure the ends of the ties. Sew
the second facing to the back panel in the same way.
Press the seams to one side and neaten the raw edges.

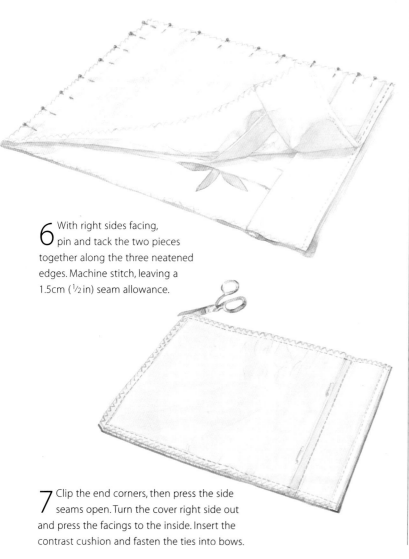

6 With right sides facing,
pin and tack the two pieces
together along the three neatened
edges. Machine stitch, leaving a
1.5cm (½in) seam allowance.

7 Clip the end corners, then press the side
seams open. Turn the cover right side out
and press the facings to the inside. Insert the
contrast cushion and fasten the ties into bows.

Pillowcase-ended cover
Materials and equipment

main fabric

cushion pad

basic sewing kit

matching sewing thread

dressmaker's pins

Measuring up and cutting out

Front and back (cut two)
width = width of pad (A)
plus 3cm (1in)
depth = depth of pad (B)
plus 3cm (1in)

Front facing
width = 12cm (5in)
depth = B plus 3cm (1in)

Back facing
width = 20cm (8in)
depth = B plus 3cm (1in)

Ties (cut four)
width = 10cm (4in)
length = 25cm (10in)

1 Attach ties and facings to
front and back pieces as for
open-ended cover up to step 5.
Press the seams open and
neaten the raw edges.

2 With right sides together,
pin and tack together
the remaining three edges
of the front and back panels.

3 Fold the (longer) back
facing across the back
panel and tack it to the
two side edges.

4 Fold the
(shorter) front
facing across the opening and
over the ties, so that it lies flat over the back
facing. Pin and tack it in place, then machine stitch
round all three edges, leaving a 1.5cm (½in) seam allowance

5 Clip the corners, then turn the cover through and press. Insert
the cushion pad, tucking it under the back facing, and knot the ties.

1 With right sides facing, pin and tack the long edge of one button panel to what will be the opening edge of the front piece. Machine stitch 1.5cm (½ in) from the edge, then press the seam allowance towards the panel. Join the second panel to the back piece in the same way.

buttoned cushion cover

A buttoned fastening can be made along one, two, three or even four sides of a cushion cover. The buttons are sewn onto the back cover and rows of buttonholes are worked on the front, parallel to the edges. The wide band of contrasting plain fabric at the opening has the effect of emphasizing the ornamental quality of the buttons.

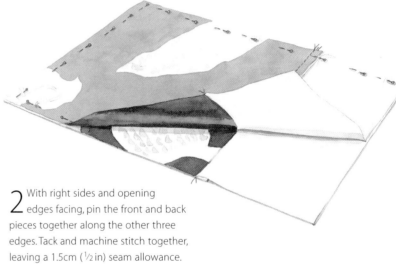

2 With right sides and opening edges facing, pin the front and back pieces together along the other three edges. Tack and machine stitch together, leaving a 1.5cm (½ in) seam allowance.

3 Clip the corners, then trim and neaten the seam allowance.

Materials and equipment

main fabric

contrast fabric

three buttons

rectangular cushion pad

basic sewing kit

matching sewing thread

dressmaker's pins

Measuring up and cutting out

Front and back pieces (cut two of each)
width = ¾ width of cushion pad (A)
plus 3cm (1in) seam allowance
depth = depth of cushion pad (B)
plus 3cm (1in) seam allowance

Button panels (cut two)
width = ½ A *plus* 3cm (1in) seam allowance
depth = B *plus* 3cm (1in) seam allowance

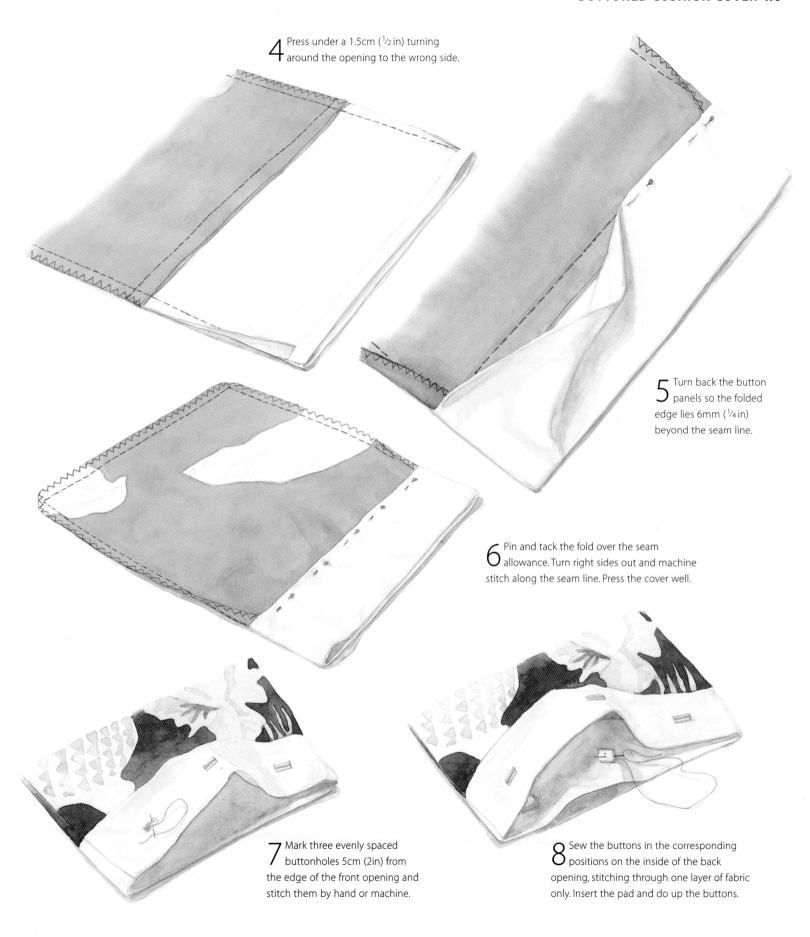

4 Press under a 1.5cm (½ in) turning around the opening to the wrong side.

5 Turn back the button panels so the folded edge lies 6mm (¼ in) beyond the seam line.

6 Pin and tack the fold over the seam allowance. Turn right sides out and machine stitch along the seam line. Press the cover well.

7 Mark three evenly spaced buttonholes 5cm (2in) from the edge of the front opening and stitch them by hand or machine.

8 Sew the buttons in the corresponding positions on the inside of the back opening, stitching through one layer of fabric only. Insert the pad and do up the buttons.

bed bolster

This bed bolster is fastened with a long zip: upholstery suppliers and good haberdashers sell zips that can be cut to a specified length. To achieve a firm, well-stuffed appearance, the cover is cut to the same size as the filling pad, without any extra seam allowance.

Materials and equipment

a 120cm (48in) length of cotton ticking or striped furnishing fabric 150cm (60in) wide

180cm (72in) medium piping cord

matching zip 30cm (12in) shorter than the length of the bolster

feather-filled bolster pad

basic sewing kit

matching sewing thread

dressmaker's pins

Measuring up and cutting out
Main piece
width = length of bolster (A)
depth = circumference of end (B)

Circular end pieces (cut two)
diameter = diameter of bolster end (C)

Piping (make two lengths)
length = C *plus* 5cm (2in)

For guidance on how to make the piping, see page 156.

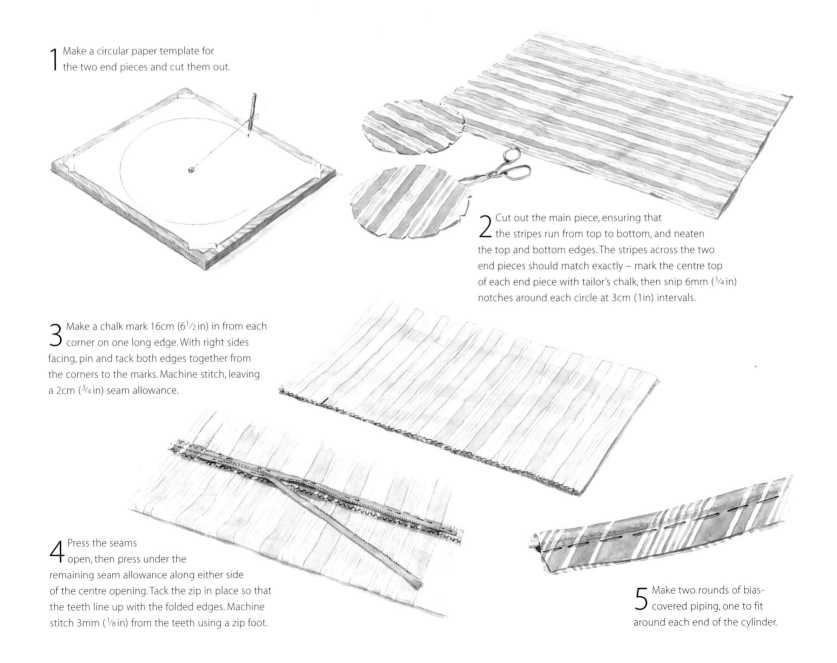

1 Make a circular paper template for the two end pieces and cut them out.

2 Cut out the main piece, ensuring that the stripes run from top to bottom, and neaten the top and bottom edges. The stripes across the two end pieces should match exactly – mark the centre top of each end piece with tailor's chalk, then snip 6mm (¼in) notches around each circle at 3cm (1in) intervals.

3 Make a chalk mark 16cm (6½in) in from each corner on one long edge. With right sides facing, pin and tack both edges together from the corners to the marks. Machine stitch, leaving a 2cm (¾in) seam allowance.

4 Press the seams open, then press under the remaining seam allowance along either side of the centre opening. Tack the zip in place so that the teeth line up with the folded edges. Machine stitch 3mm (⅛in) from the teeth using a zip foot.

5 Make two rounds of bias-covered piping, one to fit around each end of the cylinder.

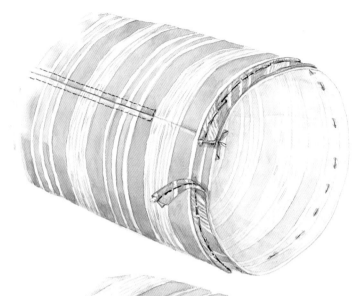

6 Pin the rounds of piping to the right side of the cover, lining up each join with the seam line.

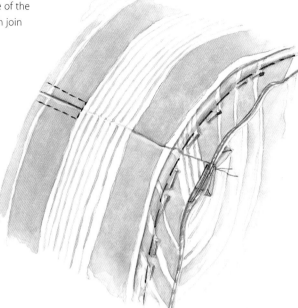

7 Neaten the joins (see page 156), then tack the rounds of piping in place. Machine stitch using a zip foot.

8 Cut a series of notches about 3cm (1in) apart into the seam allowances of both the fabric and the piping at each end of the cover. Undo the zip and turn the cover wrong side out.

9 With right sides facing, pin the circular end pieces to the open ends of the cover, matching the centre top of each to the seam line. Tack, then machine stitch close to the cord using a zip foot.

10 Trim and neaten the seam allowances. Turn right side out and press. Insert the bolster pad and close the zip.

drawstring bag

This colourful drawstring bag is simply made from a wide rectangle of fabric. The measurements can be scaled up or down to make bags of various sizes, which might be used to contain anything from the week's laundry to a pair of shoes.

Materials and equipment

105 x 80cm (41 x 31in) firm cotton fabric

1m (40in) thick piping cord

30cm (12in) striped
petersham ribbon 5cm (2in) wide

basic sewing kit

tailor's chalk

dressmaker's pins

matching sewing thread

sticky tape

safety pin

1 Fold the fabric in half widthways to find the centre point of what will be the top edge. Using tailor's chalk, mark a short line at right angles to this point on the right side of the fabric.

2 With right sides facing, fold the fabric again, then pin and tack the side and bottom edges together. Machine stitch, leaving a seam allowance of 1.5cm ($\frac{1}{2}$in), then neaten the edges. Press the side seam to one side.

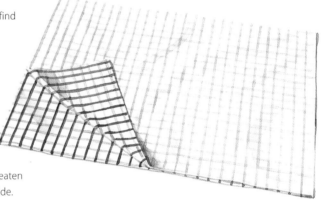

3 Press under a 1.5cm ($\frac{1}{2}$in) turning around the top edge, then press under a further 4cm (1$\frac{1}{2}$in). This will form the drawstring channel.

4 Turn the bag right side out and unfold the turnings. To make the opening for the drawstring, mark a 3cm (1$\frac{1}{4}$in) chalk line along the inner fold, across the first chalk line. Work a buttonhole by machine or hand (see page 155) along this line.

5 Turn the bag wrong side out again and refold the drawstring channel. Pin and tack the turning in place, then machine stitch close to the inner fold. Turn right side out and press.

6 Cut a 8cm (3in) length of petersham ribbon to make the toggle. Fold it in half, then pin, tack and machine stitch the two ends together, 8mm (³/₈ in) from the edge. Secure each end of the row with a few extra stitches.

7 Turn the loop of ribbon inside out carefully. Press it lightly, so that the seam lies open along the centre back. Tack along the seam line to create two channels, then work two reinforcing rows of machine stitch along this line.

8 Bind each end of the piping cord with a short length of sticky tape, then fix the safety pin to one end. Slip it through the buttonhole, then feed the cord along the drawstring channel and back out through the opening.

9 Unfasten the safety pin. Thread the ends of the piping cord through the two sides of the toggle, so that the seam lies towards the back. Cut off the sticky tape and tie the two ends together in a simple knot. Fray the ends of the cord to create a tasselled effect and trim.

10 Fold the remaining ribbon in half to make the hanging loop. Tack the two ends together and press under a turning of 1.5cm (¹/₂ in).

11 With the turning facing inwards, pin and tack the loop over the top edge of the seam line. Machine stitch in place across the bottom edge and along the top of the drawstring channel.

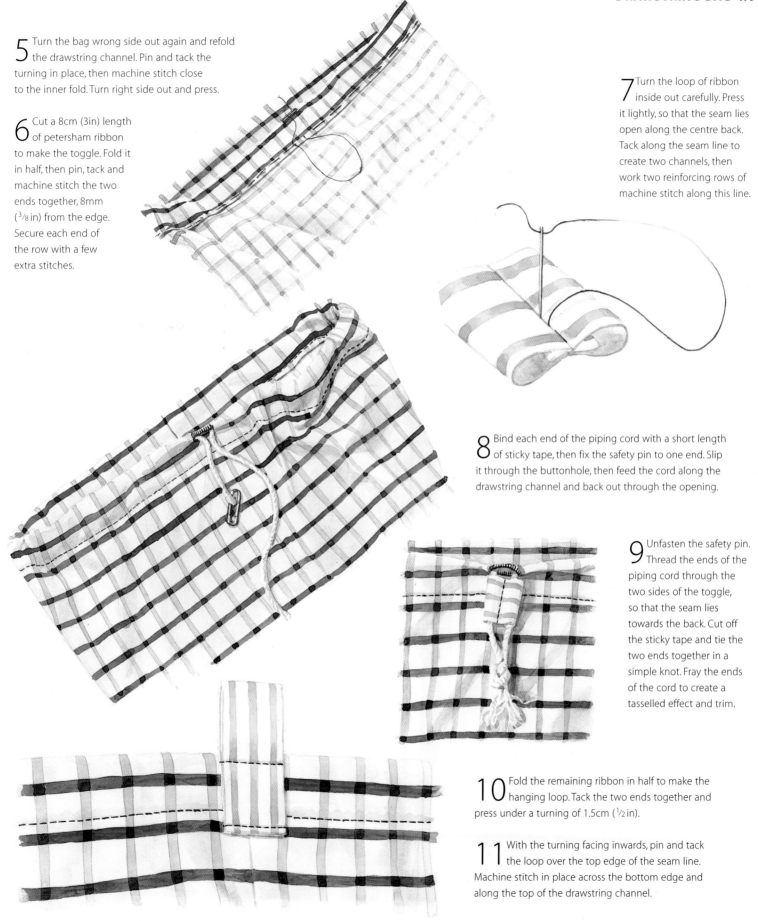

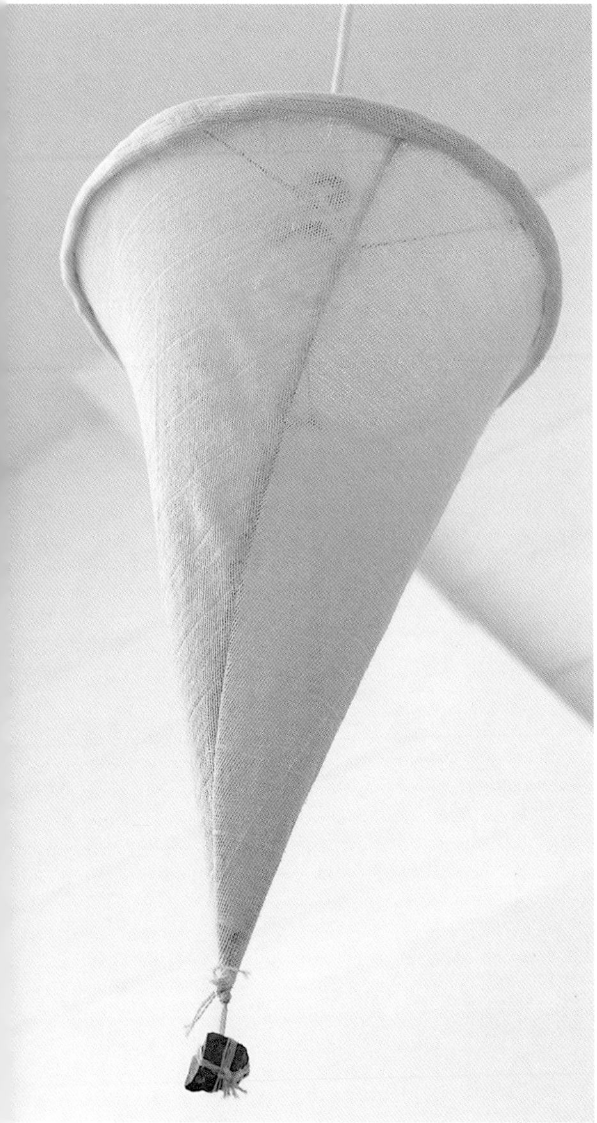

conical lampshade

This ceiling-mounted lampshade is stitched from a quarter-circle of fabric. Choose an openweave linen or cotton to create a soft, diffused effect when it is lit, and remember to use a low-watt bulb. The pebble adds a final decorative touch to the point of the cone and also helps the shade to hang properly.

materials and equipment

25cm (10in) diameter metal ring to fit over pendant light fitting

55cm (22in) square of open-weave fabric

matching sewing thread

tape measure

pencil

drawing board

masking tape

length of string and drawing pin

sheet of paper

matching bias binding

dressmaker's pins

small pebble

clear impact adhesive

tailor's chalk

ruler

Designed by Sheila Scholes

1 Start by making a semicircular template. Cut a 55cm (22in) square of paper and tape it onto a drawing board. Tie one end of the string around the pencil, near to the point, and pin the other end to one corner of the paper, so that the string is 55cm (22in) long. Holding the pencil upright, carefully draw an arc linking the two nearest corners.

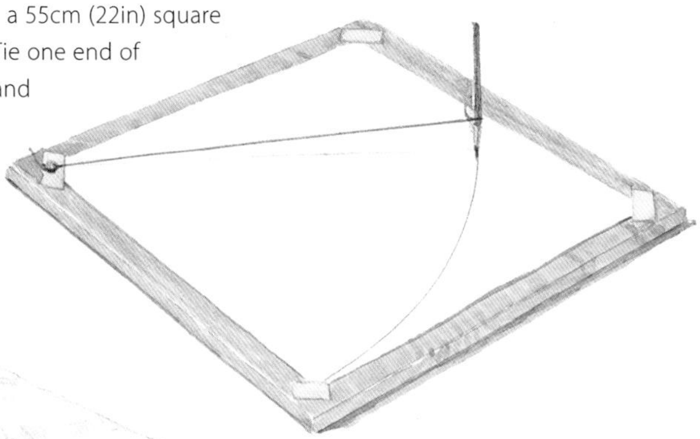

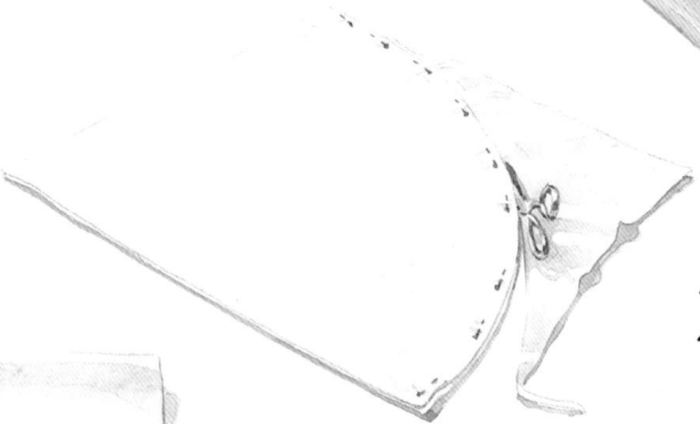

2 Cut out the template, then use this as a guide for cutting out the fabric.

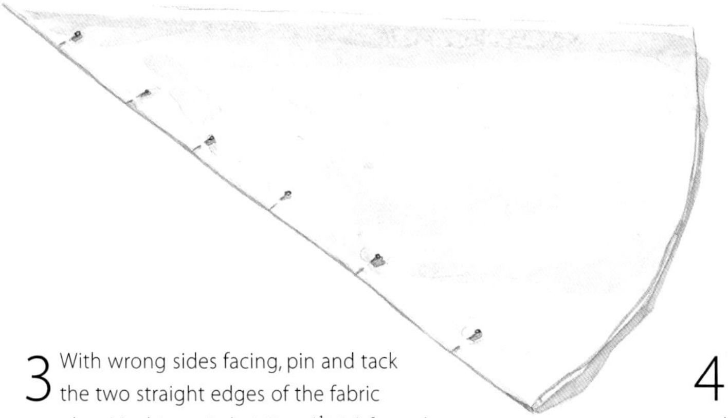

3 With wrong sides facing, pin and tack the two straight edges of the fabric together. Machine stitch, 1.5cm (½in) from the edge, then trim the seam allowance to 3mm (⅛in) and clip off the surplus fabric at the pointed end.

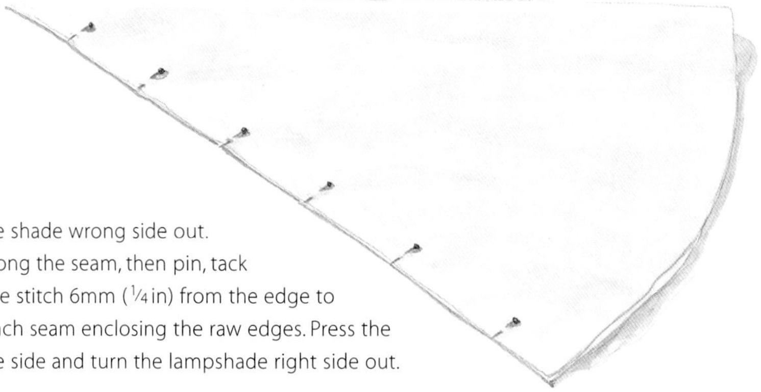

4 Turn the shade wrong side out. Press along the seam, then pin, tack and machine stitch 6mm (¼in) from the edge to make a French seam enclosing the raw edges. Press the seam to one side and turn the lampshade right side out.

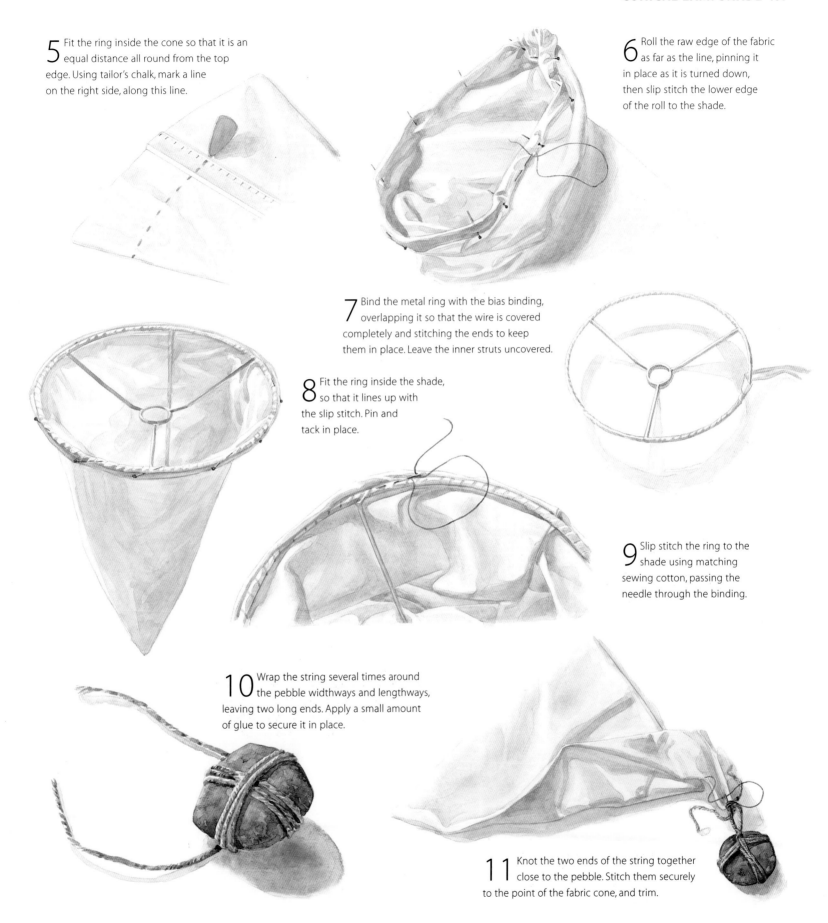

5 Fit the ring inside the cone so that it is an equal distance all round from the top edge. Using tailor's chalk, mark a line on the right side, along this line.

6 Roll the raw edge of the fabric as far as the line, pinning it in place as it is turned down, then slip stitch the lower edge of the roll to the shade.

7 Bind the metal ring with the bias binding, overlapping it so that the wire is covered completely and stitching the ends to keep them in place. Leave the inner struts uncovered.

8 Fit the ring inside the shade, so that it lines up with the slip stitch. Pin and tack in place.

9 Slip stitch the ring to the shade using matching sewing cotton, passing the needle through the binding.

10 Wrap the string several times around the pebble widthways and lengthways, leaving two long ends. Apply a small amount of glue to secure it in place.

11 Knot the two ends of the string together close to the pebble. Stitch them securely to the point of the fabric cone, and trim.

fabric basket

A square base and four rectangular sides cut from heavy cardboard are enclosed between two squares of blue gingham to make this shallow box. The size and shape could easily be varied by altering the proportions of the card pieces, to make it deeper or longer.

Materials and equipment

40 x 120cm (16 x 48in) cotton gingham

25 x 50cm (10 x 20in) cardboard 4mm (¹⁄₆ in) thick

dressmaker's scissors

craft knife

metal ruler

cutting mat

tailor's chalk

matching sewing thread

basic sewing kit

Cutting out from gingham
Front and back (cut two)
36cm (14in) square

Ties (cut eight)
width = 4cm (1¹⁄₂ in)
length = 25cm (10in)

Cutting out from cardboard
Base (cut one)
20cm (8in) square

Sides (cut four)
width = 5cm (2in)
length = 20cm (8in)

Available from Sasha Waddell

1 Press under a 2cm (³⁄₄ in) hem around each edge of the front and back cover.

2 Using tailor's chalk, mark and rule four lines on the right side of the front cover 6cm (2¹⁄₂ in) in from each folded edge.

4 Slip the cardboard base between the tacking to check that it fits snugly, then remove it and machine stitch along the two tacking lines.

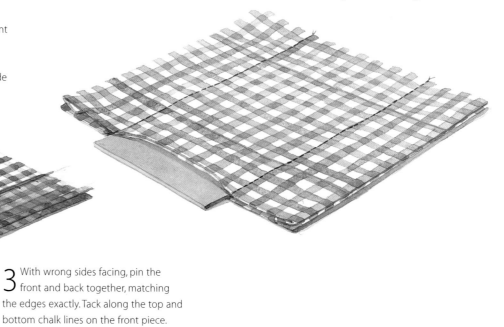

3 With wrong sides facing, pin the front and back together, matching the edges exactly. Tack along the top and bottom chalk lines on the front piece.

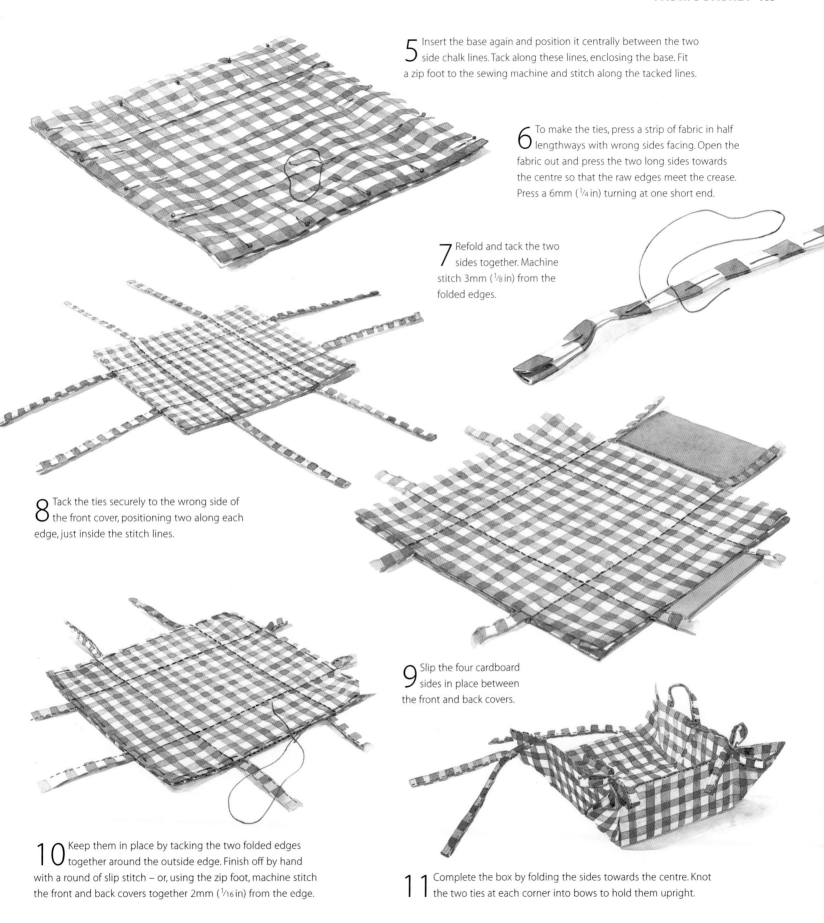

5 Insert the base again and position it centrally between the two side chalk lines. Tack along these lines, enclosing the base. Fit a zip foot to the sewing machine and stitch along the tacked lines.

6 To make the ties, press a strip of fabric in half lengthways with wrong sides facing. Open the fabric out and press the two long sides towards the centre so that the raw edges meet the crease. Press a 6mm (1/4 in) turning at one short end.

7 Refold and tack the two sides together. Machine stitch 3mm (1/8 in) from the folded edges.

8 Tack the ties securely to the wrong side of the front cover, positioning two along each edge, just inside the stitch lines.

9 Slip the four cardboard sides in place between the front and back covers.

10 Keep them in place by tacking the two folded edges together around the outside edge. Finish off by hand with a round of slip stitch – or, using the zip foot, machine stitch the front and back covers together 2mm (1/16 in) from the edge.

11 Complete the box by folding the sides towards the centre. Knot the two ties at each corner into bows to hold them upright.

Directory of suppliers

Accessories, trimmings, services

Artisan
4a Union Court
20 Union Road
London SW4 6JP
020 7627 1759
Curtain accessories, including modernist designs.

Bancroft Soft Furnishings
Brook Mill
Parker Street
Macclesfield
Cheshire SK11 7BQ
01625 615074
Sundries for curtain-making – linings, interlinings; trade only but provides list of stockists.

The Bradley Collection
Lion Barn
Maitland Road
Needham Market
Suffolk IP6 8NS
01449 722724
Contemporary and classical finials, poles, tiebacks.

Byron & Byron
Vittoria Wharf
10 Stour Road
London E3 2NT
020 8510 4800
Curtain poles and tiebacks.

Clayton Munroe
Kingston West Drive
Kingston
Staverton
Totnes
Devon TQ9 6AR
01803 762626
Curtain poles, tiebacks and stair rods.

Frances Soubeyran
12 Atlas Mews
Ramsgate Street
London E8 2NE
Handwoven passementerie.

McKinney & Co, Studio P
The Old Imperial Laundry
71 Warriner Gardens
London SW11 4XW
020 7627 5077
Finials and poles, pelmets and coronas, tiebacks, bell pulls.

Tempus Stet
Hereford House
Cranmer Road
London SW9 6EJ
020 7820 8666
Curtain accessories.

Wendy Cushing
G7, Chelsea Harbour
Design Centre
London SW10 0XE
020 8556 3555
Range of trimmings; historical restoration.

Suede and leather

Alma Home
12-14 Greatorex Street
London E1 5NF
020 7377 0762
Hides, suedes, leathers.

Connolly Leather
Orbital Park, Ashford
Kent TN24 0SA
01233 501100
Finest upholstery leather.

Evertrading Ltd
12 Martindale
East Sheen
London SW14 7AL
020 8878 4050
Range of faux fur accessories.

Mach & Garbarino
Unit K5, Cooper House
2 Michael Road
London SW6 2AD
020 7731 8555
More than 450 colours, 25 types of leather and suede from Edelman Leather.

Yarwood Leather
Treefield Industrial Estate
Gelderd Road
Morley, Leeds LS27 7JU
0113 2521014
Largest suppliers of upholstery leather to the trade; mail-order service from a single hide upwards.

Antique textiles

Ann Lister
Cam Laithe
Far Lane
Kettlewell
Skipton
North Yorks BD23 5QY
Copies of historic furnishings, fabrics and trimmings, including antique textiles.

Bryony Thomasson
19 Ackmar Road
London SW6 4UP
020 7731 3693
Handwoven sheets, covers and blankets for dyeing and furnishing.

Gallery of Antique
Costume & Textiles
2 Church Street
Marylebone
London NW8 8ED
020 7723 9981
Tapestry, needlepoint, silk, beadwork, etc, made into cushions, hangings or throws.

Jane Sacchi
7 Markham Street
London SW3 3NP
020 7589 5643
Antique French linen, tickings, table linen and cushions; by appointment.

Joanna Booth
247 Kings Road
London SW3 5EL
Early needlework, antique silks, damasks and cushions.

Judy Greenwood Antiques
657 Fulham Road
London SW6 5PY
020 7736 6037
Antique curtains, cushions, quilts and tapestries.

Lunn Antiques
86 New Kings Road
London, SW6 4LU
020 7736 4638
Textile antiques plus a range of reproduction bed linen.

Pavilion Antiques
Freshford Hall
Freshford
Bath
Somerset BA3 6EJ
Excellent stock of French linens, passementerie, trimmings; by appointment.

Port of Call
122 Ebury Street
London SW1 9QQ
020 7589 4836
Designer Mimmi O'Connell's exotic mix of antiques and modern fabrics; by appointment.

Blinds and curtains

Continental Awnings
Unit 14, Torbay Trading Est.
New Road, Brixham
Devon TQ5 8NF
01803 859996
*Blinds for exteriors and
conservatories.*

Eclectics
Unit 25, Leigh Road
Ramsgate
Kent CT12 5EU
*Modern blinds for
modern interiors.*

Faber Blinds
Kilvey Road, Brackmills
Northampton NN4 7PB
01604 766251
*Blinds and sunscreens, blind
components; wholesale only
but through stockists.*

Shades
2b Chingford Road
London E17 4PJ
Blinds made to order.

Tidmarsh & Sons
32 Hyde Way
Welwyn Garden City
Herts AL7 3AW
01707 886226
Blindmakers since 1828.

Walcot House
Lyneham Heath Studios
Lyneham, Oxon OX7 6QQ
01993 832940
*Innovative curtain hanging
systems: leather tabs, eyelet
panels, rivets and rings.*

Conservation and services

Adams & Co
The Courtyard, 24 Silver Street
Bradford on Avon
Wilts BA15 1JZ
01225 865744
*Making-up service for curtains,
blinds, pelmets, bed linen
and four-poster hangings.*

Behar Profex
The Alban Building
St Albans Place
Upper Street
London N1 0NX
020 7226 0144
*Cleaning, restoration,
de-mothing.*

Benchmark
291 Westbourne Grove
London W11 2QA
020 7229 4179
*Wide range of
upholstery studs.*

Chalfont
222 Baker Street
London NW1 5RT
020 7935 7316
*Professional dyers of
curtains, bedcovers
and loose covers.*

The Easy Chair Company
30 Lyndhurst Road
Worthing
West Sussex BN11 2DF
01903 201081
*Range of upholstery and
soft furnishing equipment
for DIY; mail order.*

Heads and Tails
Unit 11
Kingfisher Court
Hambridge Road
Newbury
Berks RG14 5SJ
01635 37730
*Curtains, pelmets, bed
hangings and headboards,
loose covers, cushions.*

Leather Conservation Centre
University College Campus
Boughton Green Road
Northampton NN2 7AN
01604 719766
*Restores and repairs screens,
leather hangings, chairs,
accessories; books and
products related to restoration
are also available.*

Let it Loose
1 Milverton Street
London SE11 4AP
020 7582 1437
*Loose covers made up,
upholstery.*

The Revival Company
The Old Stores
The Green
Great Milton
Oxon OX44 7NT
0800 393689
*Upholstery, curtain-making,
cleaning.*

Royal School of Needlework
Apartment 12a
Hampton Court Palace
Surrey KT8 9AU
020 8943 1432
*No restoration too big
or too small.*

The Suffolk Design House
Cotton Tree House
Yoxford Road
Westleton
Suffolk IP17 3AF
*Curtains, loose covers,
upholstery made up.*

Textile Conservation Centre
University of Southampton
Winchester Campus
Hants SO23 8DL
023 8059 5000
*Conservation of historically
significant textiles.*

Textile Restoration Studio
2 Talbot Road
Bowdon
Altrincham
Cheshire WA14 3JD
*Textile conservation; allied
company sells products to
preserve old fabrics.*

General suppliers

G.P. & J. Baker
PO Box 30
West End Road
High Wycombe
Bucks HP11 2QD
01494 467400
*Fabrics, faux fur cushions,
throws, from old firm
with new ideas.*

Carden Cunietti
83 Westbourne Park Road
London W2 5QH
020 7229 8630
*Designer accessories and
exclusive fabrics such
as boiled wool, feathers
and ultrasuede.*

Cath Kidston
8 Clarendon Cross
London W11 4AP
020 7221 4000
*Fabrics, oilcloth, accessories,
cushions with a modern
retro look.*

Designers Guild
3 Olaf Street
London W11 4BE
020 7243 7300
*Tricia Guild's design empire;
fabrics to throws, shops and
mail order.*

Graham & Green
10 Elgin Crescent
London W11 2JA
020 7727 4594
*Stylish throws, cushions
and notebooks.*

Laura Ashley
PO Box 5, Newtown
Powys SY16 1LX
01686 624050
*Soft furnishings with the LA
look; shops and mail order.*

John Lewis Partnership
171 Victoria Street
London SW1E 5NN
020 7828 1000
*Enormous range of home
furnishings and accessories;
25 shops with free delivery.*

Monkwell
10-12 Wharfdale Road
Bournemouth
Dorset BH4 9BT
01202 752944
*Updated throws, cushions,
cashmeres and and suede.*

Mulberry Home
Kilver Court
Shepton Mallet
Somerset BA4 5NF
01749 340500
*Fabrics, bed and table
linen, passementerie
and accessories.*

Parma Lilac
020 8960 9239
*Furnishings and accessories
especially for children's
nurseries.*

John Stefanidis
7 Friese Green House
Chelsea Manor Street
London SW3 3TW
020 7351 7511
*Fabrics and accessories
that offer a subtle mix of
classical Mediterranean
and traditional British style.*

Bed and table linen

Christy Towels
PO Box 19
Newton Street, Hyde
Cheshire SK14 4NR
0161 368 1961
*Old-established firm with
new towelling ideas.*

Damask
Broxholme House
New Kings Road
London SW6 4AA
020 7731 3553
*Updated traditional linens;
shop and mail order.*

Descamps
197 Sloane Street
London SW1X 9QX
020 7235 6957
Stylish French household linens.

Eiderdown Studio
228 Withycombe Village Road
Exmouth, Devon EX8 3BD
01395 271147
*Made-to-order bedspreads,
eiderdowns, valances,
feather mattresses.*

Fergusons Irish Linen
54 Scarva Road
Banbridge
Co. Down BT32 3AU
028 40623491
*Everything in linen
from tea towels to
damask tablecloths.*

Kirsten Hecktermann
3 Park Cottages
Campsea Ashe
Nr Woodbridge
Suffolk IP13 0QB
*Handmade cushions,
bolsters and bedspreads.*

The Holding Company
243-45 King's Road
London SW3 5EL
020 7610 9160
*A complete range of innovative
storage solutions for every room
in the home. Mail order.*

Java Cotton Company
3 Blenheim Crescent
London W11 2EE
020 9229 3212
*Hand-blocked cotton batik sold
by the metre and made up.*

Le Jacquard Francais
45 Bvd Kelsch
88402 Gerardmer
France
*Jacquard linens with
pictorial motifs.*

The Linen Cupboard
21 & 22 Great Castle Street
London W1N 7AA
020 7629 4062
*Household textiles
discounted.*

The Linen Merchant
11 Montpelier Street
London SW7 1EX
020 7584 3654
*Bed and bath linen,
embroidered and for
children.*

Melin Tregwynt
Castle Morris
Haverfordwest SA62 5UX
01348 891225
*Bedspreads, throws,
cushions, rugs, blankets
from Welsh mill.*

Old Town
49 Bull Street
Holt, Norfolk NR25 6HP
01263 710001
*Quilt and pillow covers in old-
fashioned textiles – gingham,
ticking and tartan.*

Snap Dragon
247 Fulham Road
London SW3 6HY
020 7376 8889
*Eastern antiques and
contemporary interpretations.*

Souleiado
Z.I. de Roubian
13150 Tarascon
France
*Traditional Provençal
fabrics and accessories.*

Volga Linen Company
Unit 1D
Eastland Road
Industrial Estate
Leiston
Suffolk IP16 4LL
01728 635020
*Bed and table linen actually in
100% linen imported from Russia.*

The White Company
Unit 30
Perivale Industrial Park
Horsenden Lane South
Greenford UB6 7RJ
020 8799 6700
*Fast mail order of
bed and table linen
plus accessories.*

Fabrics
Anna French
343 Kings Road
London SW3 5ES
020 7737 6555
*Extensive range of patterned
cottons and sheers.*

Anta
32 Royal Mile
Edinburgh EH1 1TB
0131 557 8300
*Tartan fabrics and
accessories.*

ARC
103 Wandsworth Bridge Road
London SW6 2TE
020 7731 3933
*Print-maker now making
print-room fabrics.*

Belinda Coote Tapestries
Unit 3/14, Chelsea Harbour
   Design Centre
London SW10 0XE
020 7351 0404
*Tapestries by the metre;
cushions, throws and borders.*

Bennison Fabrics
10 Holbein Place
London SW1W 8NL
020 7730 8076
*King of tea-stains and muted
18th-century fabrics.*

Bentley & Spens
1-2 Mornington Street
London NW1 7QD
020 7387 7374
*Sparky modern fabrics,
along with making-up
service and design advice.*

Bernard Thorp
53 Chelsea Manor Street
London SW3 5RZ
020 7352 5457
*Designs printed to your
colours.*

Colefax and Fowler
39 Brook Street
London W1Y 2JE
020 7493 2231
*Famous fabrics and etcs from
the school of John Fowler.*

The Conran Shop
Michelin House
81 Fulham Road
London SW3 6RD
020 7589 7401
*Cutting-edge fabrics
and accessories.*

Fired Earth
Twyford Mill
Oxford Road, Adderbury
Oxon OX17 3HP
01295 814399
*Newly diversified from
tiles into archive fabrics.*

Heal's
196 Tottenham Court Road
London W1P 9LD
020 7636 1666 for branches
*A wide range of
contemporary fabrics.*

George Spencer Decorations
29 Chapel Street
London SW1X 7DD
020 7235 1501
*Naturals, neutrals, and
textured fabrics.*

The Humphries Weaving Co.
DeVere Mill
Castle Hedingham
Halstead
Essex CO9 3HA
01787 461193
*Handloomed silks and historic
fabrics; designs made to order.*

Holland & Sherry
PO Box 1
Venlaw Road
Peebles
Borders EH45 8RN
01721 720101
*Luxury cloth weavers for fashion
and decorative trades.*

Ian Mankin
109 Regents Park Road
London NW1 8UR
020 7722 0997
*Stripes and tickings regularly
updated; also mail order.*

The Isle Mill
Tower House
Ruthvenfield Road
Inveralmond
Perth PH1 3UN
01738 609090
*Luxury natural fabrics;
specializing neutrals
and textured fabrics.*

Jane Churchill
151 Sloane Street
London SW1X 9BX
020 7730 9847
*Updated traditional
fabrics and accessories.*

John Boyd Textiles
Higher Flax Mills
Castle Cary
Somerset BA7 7DY
01963 350 451
*One of only two horsehair
weavers left in Europe –
terrific stuff; trade only
but stockists given.*

Lelievre
1/19 Chelsea Harbour
   Design Centre
Chelsea Harbour
London SW10 0XE
020 7352 4798
*Velvets, silks, damask, fur
effects, prints.*

Lewis & Wood
5 The Green
Uley
Nr Dursley
Glos GL11 5SN
01453 860080
*Heavyweight plain linens
for curtains, upholstery.*

Manuel Canovas
2 North Terrace
London SW3 2BA
020 7225 2298
*Elegantly coloured fabrics
by master designer.*

Natural Fabric Co.
127 High Street
Hungerford
Berks RG17 0Dl
01488 684002
*Fine range, from toile
to tartan.*

Nina Campbell
7 Milner Street
London SW3 2QA
020 7589 8589
Rich prints; Scottish themes.

Pierre Frey
251-253 Fulham Road
London SW3 6HY
020 7376 5599
*Also represents Declercq
passementerie, Etro and
Philippe Hurel.*

Pongees
28-30 Hoxton Square
London N1 6NN
020 7739 9130
*Huge variety of silks, satins,
georgettes, plus dyeing.*

Osborne & Little
304 Kings Road
London SW3 5UH
020 7352 1456
Still innovating after 30 years.

Simply Scandinavian
Nielsen McNally
6 Eggars Hill
Aldershot
Hants GU11 3NQ
*Represents Marimekko and
Saldo fabrics; mail order.*

Simon Playle
6 Fulham Park Studios
London SW6 4LW
020 7371 0131
American fabrics, voiles.

Stuart
Barrington Court
Barrington, Ilminster
Somerset TA19 0NQ
01460 240349
Reproductions of historic textiles.

Timney Fowler
388 Kings Road
London SW3 5UZ
020 7352 2263
*Classic prints reworked
and recoloured.*

Thomas Dare
11 &12 Saxon Business Centre
Windsor Avenue
London SW19 2RR
020 8542 1160
Spirited pictorials.

Architects and designers whose work is featured in this book

Ash Sakula Architects
Studio 115
38 Mount Pleasant
London WC1X 0AN
020 7837 9735
Pages 1, 67 al

Benchmark Group plc
25 Sackville Street
London W1
Pages 9, 18-19, 26 & 27 l, 79
bl, 98 l, 122 ar & br

Charlotte Barnes Interiors
26 Stanhope Gardens
London SW7 5QX
Pages 70 l

JoAnn Barwick
Interior Designer
P.O. Box 982
Boca Grande, FL 33921
USA
Pages 38 br, 114-115

Bilhuber Inc.
330 East 59th Street, 6th fl.
New York, NY 10022
USA
+ 1 212 308 4888
Pages 92 al, 110-111

Blakes Lodging
77 Pantigo Road
East Hampton
New York, NY 11937
USA
+1 631 324 1815
www.picket.com
Pages 59, 66 l, 79 bc, 84,
132-133, 148

Laura Bohn Design
30 West 26th Street
New York, NY 10010
USA
+1 212 645 3636
www.laurabohndesign.
  com
Pages 13 r, 22-23, 45, 86 b,
87 br, 92 bl, 122, bl, 137, 164

Ann Boyd Design Ltd
33 Elystan Street
London SW3 3NT
020 7591 0202
Pages 15 al, 76 bc, 86 cr,
87 l, 111 a

Nancy Braithwaite Interiors
2300 Peachtree Road
Atlanta, GA 30309
USA
Page 64

Sabina Fay Braxton
Cloth of Gold
Grennan Watermill
Thomastown
Co Kilkenny
Ireland
+353 565 4383
by appointment in New York:
+1 212 535 2587
by appointment in Paris:
+33 1 46 57 11 62
Pages 25 r, 68 a, 71 a,
82 a, 86 a & cl, 94 b, 103 al,
142 a

Clive Butcher Designs
The Granary
The Quay
Wivenhoe
Essex CO7 9BU
01206 827708
Page 138

Piero Castellini Baldissera
Studio Castellini
Via Morozzo della
  Rocco, 5
20123 Milan
Italy
Pages 97 a

David Collins
  Architecture & Design
Unit 6 & 7
Chelsea Wharf
Lots Road
London SW10 0QJ
020 7349 5900
Pages 27 ar, 74, 83 al, 98 r

Conner Prairie Musuem
134000 Alisonville Road
Fishers, IN 46038
USA
Page 128 l

Chris Cowper
Cowper Griffith Associates
Chartered Architects
15 High Street
Whittlesford
Cambridge CB2 4LT
Page 129 r

Jo Crepain
  Architect
Vlaandernstraat 6
8-2000 Antwerp
Belgium
+32 3 213 61 61
Page 93 bl

CR Studio Architects, PC
6 West 18th Street, 9th fl.
New York, NY 10011
+1 212 989 8187
www.crstudio.com
Pages 34, 76 bl, 77, 79 ar &
br, 99 al & r, 122 al

John Cullen Lighting
585 King's Road
London SW6 2EH
020 7371 5400
Page 103, ar

De Le Cuona Textile and
  Home Collection
Head Office:
9-10 Osborne Mews
Windsor
Berks SL4 3DE

Retail outlet:
De Le Cuona, 1st fl.
The General Trading Co.
2 Symons Street
London SW3 2TJ
www.delecuona.co.uk
Pages 15 bl, 16 l, 80 br,
90 cc, 139 l

Mary Drysdale
1733 Connecticut Avenue
  NW,
Washington DC 20009
USA
Pages 11 a, 150 r, 152, 168

Ecomusée de la Grande
  Lande
Marquèze
40630 Sabres
Bordeaux, France
Page 131

Han Feng
Fashion designer
333 West 39 Street, 12th fl.
New York, NY 10018
USA
+1 212 695 9509
Page 140 bl & br

Ken Foreman
  Architect
105 Duane Street
New York, NY 10007
USA
+1 212 924 4503
Pages 35, 68 b, 83 ac & ar,
108 l & 108-109

Mark Gillette
  Interior Design
The Barn, Elthorns Farm
Denhall Lane
Burton
South Wirral
Cheshire CH64 5SA
0151 336 3528
mark.gillette@
  breathemail.net
Pages 27 cr, 65 a
*Favours the use of natural,
textured surfaces and
finishes including limestone,
oak, linen and suede.*

Zina Glazebrook
ZG DESIGN
10 Wireless Road
East Hampton
NY 11937
USA
+1 631 329 7486
www.zgdesign.com
Page 75 al

James Gorst Architects
35 Lambs Conduit Street
London WC1N 3NG
020 7831 8300
Pages 119 b, 10 l

Wendy Harrop
Interior Designer
11 Rectory Road
London SW13 0DU
Pages 50-51 67 br, 112,
126 a

Hi-Tex Inc.
Crypton Super Fabric
32813 Middlebelt
Farmington Hills
MI 48334
USA
+1 1 800 CRYPTON
www.cryptonfabric.com
Pages 34, 76 bl, 77, 79 ar &
br, 99 al & r, 122 al

John C Hope
  Architects
3 St Bernard's Crescent
Edinburgh EH4 1NR
0131 315 2215
Page 123 l

Interni Pty Ltd
Interior Design
  Consultancy
15-19 Boundary Street
Rushcutter's Bay
Sydney 2010
Australia
Page 63

IPL Interiors
François Gilles and
Dominique Lubar
Unit 26C1
Thames House
140 Battersea Park Road
London SW11 4NY
020 7622 3009
Page 127

Jacomini Interior Design
1701 Brun
Suite 101
Houston, TX
USA
Pages 96 ar, 126 b

Joanna Jefferson
  Architects
222 Oving Road
Chichester
West Sussex PO19 4EJ
01243 532 398
jjeffearch@aol.com
Page 123 r

Johnson Naylor
13 Britton Street
London EC1M 5SX
020 7490 8885
Page 90 cl

McDowell + Benedetti
  Architects
62 Rosebery Avenue
London EC1R 4RR
020 7278 8810
McDowellBenedetti.com
Page 69

MODÉNATURE
Créations Henry Becq
3, rue Jacob
  et 59, rue de Seine
75006 Paris, France
Pages 29 al & br, 56, 80 a,
106 & 107 a, 118, 135 bl,
c & r, 184

Lynn Morgan Design
19 Hilltop Road
Norwalk
CT 06854
USA
+1 203 854 5037
Pages 12-13, 36-37, 38 bl,
95 b, 117, 146-147

Claire Nelson
Nelson Design
169 St Johns Hill
London SW11 1TQ
020 7924 4542
Pages 9, 18-19, 26 & 27 l, 79
bl, 98 l, 122 ar & br

Roger Oates Design
Shop & Showroom:
1 Munro Terrace
off Cheyne Walk
London SW10 0DL

Studio shop:
The Long Barn
Eastnor
Ledbury
Herefordshire HR8 1EL

*Rugs and runners
mail order catalogue:*
01531 631611
Pages 10 r, 15 ar, 30 al,
72 l, 121, 140 ar, 141

Ogawa/Depardon
  Architects
137 Varick Street, #404
New York
NY 10013
USA
+1 212 627 7390
Page 55

OKA Direct
A unique collection of mail order furniture and home accessories including rattan, painted furniture, leather and horn.
For a catalogue, please call 0870 160 6002
www.okadirect.com
Pages 27 br, 29 bl, 54 b, 83 br, 103 b, 120, 134 & 135 a, 192

Andrew Parr
SJB Interior Design Pty Ltd.
Studio Southbank
5 Haig Street
South Melbourne 3205
Australia
Page 62 l

Caroline Paterson
Paterson Gornall Interiors
50 Lavender Gardens
London SW11 1DN
020 7738 2530
Pages 92 br, 138

Plain English
Kitchen Design
The Tannery
Coombs
Stowmarket
Suffolk IP14 2EN
Page 129 bl

Lena Proudlock
Furniture Design 12
Gloucestershire GL8 8UN
Page 125 l

Mark Pynn A.I.A.
McMillen Pynn
  Architecture L.L.P.
P.O. Box 1068
Sun Valley
ID 83353
USA
+1 208 622 4656
www.sunvalleyarchitect.
  com
Page 16 r

Reed Creative Services Ltd
151a Sydney Street
London SW3 6NT
020 7565 0066
Pages 15 al, 76 bc, 103 ar, 111 a

Johanne Riss
Stylist, Designer &
  Fashion Designer
35 Place du Nouveau
Marché aux Graens
1000 Brussels
Belgium
+32 2 513 0900
Pages 14, 93 al

Richard Ronald
c/o Manuel Canovas
2 North Terrace
London SW3
Page 7

Steven Ryan
Design and Decoration
60 Ledbury Road
London W11
020 7488 0555
Page 44 br

Sheila Scholes, Designer
01480 498241
Pages 5, 28 l, 59 b, 70 r, 80 bl, 81, 88-89, 100 l, 101 l & r, 128 r, 132 a, 144 l, 180

Sequana
64 Avenue de la Motte
  Picquet
75015 Paris, France
+33 1 45 66 58 40
sequana@wanadoo.fr
Pages 20 ac, b & 21, 111 b

Taylor Woodrow Capital
  Developments Ltd
International House
1 St Katherine's Way
London E1 9TW
020 7488 0555
Pages 27 ar, 74, 83 al, 98 r

Todhunter Earle Interiors
Chelsea Reach
1st fl., 79-89 Lots Road
London SW10 0RN
020 7349 9999
www.todhunterearle.com
Pages 29 ar, 61 a, 107 b, 119 a, 144 r

Sasha Waddell
269 Wandsworth Bridge
  Road
London SW6 2TX
020 7736 0766
Pages 2-3, 32 a & b, 39, 59 ar, 65 b, 72 r, 78, 79 al & cl, 90 b, 182

Picture credits

Key: *a* = above, *b* = below, *l* = left, *r* = right, *c* = centre
All photographs by David Montgomery unless otherwise stated
Endpapers photographer Polly Wreford; **1** photographer James Merrell/An apartment in London designed by Ash Sakula Architects; **2-3** Sasha Waddell's house in London; **4** photographer Tom Leighton; **5** Sheila Scholes' house near Cambridge; **7** photographer James Merrell/Richard Ronald's house in London; **8-9** Carlton Gardens apartment in London designed by Claire Nelson at Nelson Design; **10** *l* photographer Andrew Wood/An apartment in London designed by James Gorst; **10** *r* photographer Andrew Wood/Roger Oates & Fay Morgan's house in Eastnor; **11** *a* photographer James Merrell/A house designed by Mary Drysdale; **11** *b* photographer Simon Upton/Carol Reid's apartment in Paris; **12-13** A house in Connecticut designed by Lynn Morgan Design; **13** *r* photographer Fritz von der Schulenburg/A house in Pennsylvania designed by Laura Bohn of Laura Bohn Design Associates; **14** photographer Andrew Wood/Johanne Riss' house in Brussels; **15** *al* photographer James Merrell/Designed by Reed Boyd; **15** *ar* photographer Tom Leighton/Roger Oates & Fay Morgan's house in Eastnor; **15** *bl* photographer Andrew Wood/Bernie de Le Cuona's house in Windsor; **15** *br* photographer James Merrell; **16** *l* photographer Andrew Wood/Bernie de Le Cuona's house in Windsor; **16** *r* photographer Andrew Wood/Philip & Barbara Silver's house in Idaho designed by McMillen Pynn Architecture; **17** photographer James Merrell; **18-19** Carlton Gardens apartment in London designed by Claire Nelson at Nelson Design; **20** *al* photographer Sandra Lane; **20** *ac, b* & **21** photographer Andrew Wood/Mary Shaw's Sequana apartment in Paris; **20** *ar* photographer Tom Leighton; **22-23** Laura Bohn's apartment in New York designed by Laura Bohn Design Associates; **24** *l* & *ar* photographer James Merrell; **24** *br* photographer James Merrell; **25** *l* photographer James Merrell/Liz Dougherty Pierce's home; **25** *r* Sabina Fay Braxton's apartment in Paris; **26** & **27** *l* Carlton Gardens apartment in London designed by Claire Nelson at Nelson Design; **27** *ar* The Montevetro apartment in London designed by David Collins, photographed courtesy of Taylor Woodrow Capital Developments Ltd.; **27** *cr* The Nobilis-Fontan apartment in London designed by Mark Gillette; **27** *br* Annabel Astor's house in London is full of furniture and accessories designed exclusively for her OKA Direct Mail

order catalogue; **28** *l* Sheila Scholes' house near Cambridge; **28** *r* & **29** *ar* House in South London designed by Todhunter Earle Interiors; **29** *al* & *br* Designer of Modénature Henry Becq's apartment in Paris; **29** *bl* Annabel Astor's house in London is full of furniture and accessories designed exclusively for her OKA Direct Mail order catalogue; **30** *al* photographer Henry Bourne/Roger Oates & Fay Morgan's house in Eastnor; **30** *bl* photographer Simon Upton; **30** *r* photographer James Merrell/Høyersten family house on western fiord in Norway; **31** *al, ac, bl* & *br* photographer James Merrell; **31** *ar* photographer Henry Bourne; **32** *a* & *b* Sasha Waddell's house in London; **33** photographer James Merrell/Hotel Villa Gallici Aix en Provence, France; **34** The House of Crypton living laboratory apartment showroom in New York City designed by CR Studio Architects, PC; **35** An apartment in New York designed by Ken Foreman; **36-37** A house in Connecticut designed by Lynn Morgan Design; **38** *bl* A house in Connecticut designed by Lynn Morgan Design; **38** *a* photographer Polly Wreford/The Sawmills Studios; **38** *br* photographer Simon Upton/JoAnn Barwick & Fred Berger's house in New Preston, Connecticut; **39** Sasha Waddell's house in London; **40** *a* & *b* photographer Tom Leighton; **41** *a* photographer Polly Wreford; **41** *bl* photographer Polly Wreford/Mary Foley's house in Connecticut; **41** *br* photographer Polly Wreford; **42-43** photographer James Merrell/Hotel de la Mirande, Avignon; **44** *al* & *bl* photographer James Merrell/Ngila Boyd, London; **44** *ar* photographer James Merrell/Hotel Villa Gallici Aix en Provence, France; **44** *br* photographer James Merrell/Interior Design by Stephen Ryan Design & Decoration; **45** Laura Bohn's apartment in New York designed by Laura Bohn Design Associates; **46** photographer James Merrell/Hotel Villa Gallici Aix en Provence, France; **47** & **48** photographer James Merrell/Hotel de la Mirande, Avignon; **49** & **50** *l* photographer James Merrell; **50-51** photographer Simon Upton/Wendy Harrop's cottage in Wiltshire; **52-53** photographer Tom Leighton; **54** *a* photographer James Merrell/Curtain design Mary Bright; **54** *b* Annabel Astor's house in London is full of furniture and accessories designed exclusively for her OKA Direct Mail order catalogue; **55** photographer James Merrell/Architect Ogawa Depardon, curtain design Mary Bright; **56** Designer of Modénature Henry Becq's apartment in Paris; **57** *l* photographer James Merrell/Hotel de la Mirande, Avignon; **57** *ar* & *br* photographer

James Merrell; **58** *a* photographer James Merrell; **59** *b* photographer Simon Upton/Maison d'Hôte; **59** Blakes Lodging designed by Jeanie Blake www.picket.com/blakesBB/blakes.htm; **59** *ar* Sasha Waddell's house in London; **59** *b* Sheila Scholes' house near Cambridge; **60** *bl* & **60-61** photographer James Merrell; **61** *a* House in South London designed by Todhunter Earle Interiors; **62** *l* photographer James Merrell/Andrew Parr's house in Melbourne; **62** *r* photographer Henry Bourne; **63** photographer James Merrell/A house in Sydney designed by Interni Interior Design Consultancy; **64** photographer Simon Upton/Nancy Braithwaite Interiors; **65** *a* the Nobilis-Fontan apartment in London designed by Mark Gillette; **65** *b* Sasha Waddell's house in London; **66** *l* Blakes Lodging designed by Jeanie Blake www.picket.com/blakesBB/blakes.htm; **66** *r* photographer Ray Main/Nello Renault's loft in Paris; **67** *al* photographer Ray Main; **67** *ar* photographer James Merrell/An apartment in London designed by Ash Sakula Architects; **67** *bl* photographer Simon Upton/Mr & Mrs Ruttenberg's house in Pennsylvania; **67** *br* photographer Simon Upton/Wendy Harrop's cottage in Wiltshire; **68** *a* Sabina Fay Braxton's apartment in Paris; **68** *b* An apartment in New York designed by Ken Foreman; **69** photographer Ray Main/David & Claudia Dorrell's apartment in London designed in conjunction with McDowell + Benedetti; **70** *l* photographer James Merrell/Designer Charlotte Barnes; **70** *r* Sheila Scholes' house near Cambridge; **71** *a* Sabina Fay Braxton's apartment in Paris; **71** *b* photographer Fritz von der Schulenburg/Jason McCoy's apartment in New York; **72** *l* photographer Tom Leighton/Roger Oates & Fay Morgan's house in Eastnor; **72** *r* Sasha Waddell's house in London; **73** photographer Polly Wreford/Kimberly Watson's house in London; **74** The Montevetro apartment in London designed by David Collins, photographed courtesy of Taylor Woodrow Capital Developments Ltd; **75** *al* photographer Ray Main/Client's residence, East Hampton, New York, designed by ZG DESIGN; **75** *ar* photographer James Merrell; **75** *br* photographer Henry Bourne; **76** *a* photographer Tom Leighton; **76** *bl* The House of Crypton living laboratory apartment showroom in New York City designed by CR Studio Architects, PC; **76** *bc* photographer Tom Leighton/Keith Varty & Alan Cleaver's apartment in London designed by Jonathan Reed/Reed Boyd; **76** *br* photographer Tom Leighton/Arne Maynard; **77** The House of Crypton living laboratory apartment showroom in New York City designed by CR Studio Architects, PC; **78, 79** *al* & *cl* Sasha Waddell's house in London; **79** *bl* Carlton Gardens apartment in London designed by Claire Nelson at Nelson Design; **79** *bc* Blakes Lodging designed by Jeanie Blake www.picket.com/blakesBB/blakes.htm; **79** *ar* & *br* The House of Crypton living laboratory apartment showroom in New York City designed by CR Studio Architects, PC; **80** *a* Designer of Modénature Henry Becq's apartment in Paris; **80** *bl* Sheila Scholes' house near Cambridge; **80** *br* photographer Andrew Wood/Bernie de Le Cuona's house in Windsor; **81** Sheila Scholes' house near Cambridge; **82** *a* Sabina Fay Braxton's apartment in Paris; **82** *b* photographer James Merrell; **83** *al* The Montevetro apartment in London designed by David Collins, photographed courtesy of Taylor Woodrow Capital Developments Ltd; **83** *ac* & *ar* An apartment in New York designed by Ken Foreman; **83** *bl* photographer Polly Wreford/Ros Fairman's house in London; **83** *br* Annabel Astor's house in London is full of furniture and accessories designed exclusively for her OKA Direct Mail order catalogue; **84** Blakes Lodging designed by Jeanie Blake www.picket.com/blakesBB/blakes.htm; **85** *l* photographer Polly Wreford/Adria Ellis' apartment in New York; **85** *r* photographer James Merrell; **86** *a* & *cl* Sabina Fay Braxton's apartment in Paris; **86** *b* Laura Bohn's apartment in New York designed by Laura Bohn Design Associates; **86** *cr* & **87** *l* photographer James Merrell/Anne Boyd; **87** *ar* photographer Tom Leighton; **87** *br* Laura Bohn's apartment in New York designed by Laura Bohn Design Associates; **88-89** Sheila Scholes' house near Cambridge; **90** *a* photographer James Merrell/Janie Jackson, Stylist/Desginer; **90** *cl* photographer Andrew Wood/Roger & Suzy Black's apartment in London designed by Johnson Naylor; **90** *c* photographer Andrew Wood/Bernie de Le Cuona's house in Windsor; **90** *cr* photographer James Merrell; **90** *b* Sasha Waddell's house in London; **91** *a* photographer Henry Bourne; **91** *b* photographer Polly Wreford; **92** *al* photographer Ray Main/A house in Pennsylvania designed by Jeffrey Bilhuber; **92** *bl* photographer Fritz von der Schulenburg/A house in Pennsylvania designed by Laura Bohn of Laura Bohn Design Associates; **92** *br* photographer Fritz von der Schulenburg/Philippa Rose's apartment in London designed by Caroline Paterson with furniture supplied by Leonie Lee of Snap Dragon; **93** *al* photographer Andrew Wood/Johanne Riss' house in Brussels; **93** *bl* photographer Andrew Wood/Architect Jo Crepain; **93** *r* photographer James Merrell/Janie Jackson, Stylist/Desginer; **94** *a* photographer Simon Upton; **94** *b* Sabina Fay Braxton's apartment in Paris; **95** *a* photographer Henry Bourne/Ellen O'Neill, Sag Harbour, New York; **95** *b* A house in Connecticut designed by Lynn Morgan Design; **96** *al* & *bl* photographer James Merrell; **96** *ar* photographer Simon Upton/Jacomini Interior Design; **97** *a* photographer Fritz von der Schulenburg/Piero Castellini Baldissera's house in Montalcino, Siena; **97** *b* photographer James Merrell; **98** *l* Carlton Gardens apartment in London designed by Claire Nelson at Nelson Design; **98** *r* The Montevetro apartment in London designed by David Collins, photographed courtesy of Taylor Woodrow Capital Developments Ltd; **99** *al* & *r* The House of Crypton living laboratory apartment showroom in New York City designed by CR Studio Architects, PC; **99** *b* photographer James Merrell; **100** *l*, **101** *l* & *r* Sheila Scholes' house near Cambridge; **100** *r* photographer Sandra Lane; **102** photographer James Merrell; **103** *al* Sabina Fay Braxton's apartment in Paris; **103** *ar* photographer Ray Main/Jonathan Reed's apartment in London, lighting designed by Sally Storey, Design Director of John Cullen Lighting; **103** *b* Annabel Astor's house in London is full of furniture and accessories designed exclusively for her OKA Direct Mail order catalogue; **104-105** photographer Andrew Wood/Gabriele Sanders' apartment in New York; **106** & **107** *a* Designer of Modénature Henry Becq's apartment in Paris; **107** *b* House in South London designed by Todhunter Earle Interiors; **108** *l* & **108-109** An apartment in New York designed by Ken Foreman; **110-111** photographer Ray Main/A house in Pennsylvania designed by Jeffrey Bilhuber; **111** *a* photographer James Merrell/Keith Varty & Alan Cleaver's apartment in London designed by Jonathan Reed/Reed & Boyd; **111** *b* photographer Andrew Wood/Mary Shaw's Sequana apartment in Paris; **112** photographer Simon Upton/Wendy Harrop's cottage in Wiltshire; **113** Zara Colchester's house in London; **114-115** photographer Simon Upton/JoAnn Barwick & Fred Berger's house in New Preston, Connecticut; **115** *r* & **116** photographer Henry Bourne; **117** A house in Connecticut designed by Lynn Morgan Design; **118** Designer of Modénature Henry Becq's apartment in Paris; **119** *a* House in South London designed by Todhunter Earle Interiors; **119** *b* photographer Andrew Wood/an apartment in London designed by James Gorst; **120** Annabel Astor's house in London is full of furniture and accessories designed exclusively for her OKA Direct Mail order catalogue; **121** photographer Andrew Wood/Roger Oates & Fay Morgan's house in Eastnor; **122** *al* The House of Crypton living laboratory apartment showroom in New York City designed by CR Studio Architects, PC; **122** *bl* Laura Bohn's apartment in New York designed by Laura Bohn Design Associates; **122** *ar* & *br* Carlton Gardens apartment in London designed by Claire Nelson at Nelson Design; **123** *l* photographer Ray Main/Robert Callender & Elizabeth Ogilvie's studio in Fife designed by John C Hope Architects; **123** *r* photographer Ray Main/Marina & Peter Hill's barn in West Sussex designed by Marina Hill, Peter James Construction Management, Chichester, The West Sussex Antique Timber Company, Wisborough Green, and Joanna Jefferson Architects; **124** photographer James Merrell/ Gabriele Sanders' apartment in New York; **125** *l* photographer Polly Wreford/Lena Proudlock's house in Gloucestershire; **125** *r* photographer Polly Wreford/Kimberly Watson's house in London; **126** *a* photographer Simon Upton/

Wendy Harrop's cottage in Wiltshire; **126** *b* photographer Simon Upton/Jacomini Interior Design; **127** photographer Simon Upton/A house in Tangier designed by François Gilles of IPL Interiors; **128** *l* photographer Simon Upton/Conner Prairie Museum; **128** *r* Sheila Scholes' house near Cambridge; **129** *a* photographer Tom Leighton; **129** *bl* photographer Simon Upton/A kitchen designed by Plain English; **129** *r* photographer Simon Upton/ A house in Norfolk designed by Chris Cowper of Cowper Griffith Associates, Chartered Architects; **130** photographer Henry Bourne; **131** photographer Simon Upton/Ecomusée de la Grande Lande; **131** *b* photographer James Merrell/Høyersten family house on western fiord in Norway; **132** *a* Sheila Scholes' house near Cambridge; **132** *b* & **132-133** Blakes Lodging designed by Jeanie Blake www.picket.com/blakesBB/blakes.htm; **134** & **135** *a* Annabel Astor's house in London is full of furniture and accessories designed exclusively for her OKA Direct Mail order catalogue; **135** *bl, c* & *r* Designer of Modénature Henry Becq's apartment in Paris; **136** photographer Andrew Wood/Dawna and Jerry Walter's house in London; **137** Laura Bohn's apartment in New York designed by Laura Bohn Design Associates; **138** photographer Chris Everard/Philippa Rose's house in London designed by Caroline Paterson/Victoria Fairfax of Paterson Gornall Interiors, together with Clive Butcher Designs; **139** *l* photographer Andrew Wood/Bernie de Le Cuona's house in Windsor; **139** *r* photographer James Merrell; **140** *ar* photographer Andrew Wood/ Roger Oates & Fay Morgan's house in Eastnor; **140** *bl* & *br* photographer Andrew Wood/Han Feng's apartment in New York designed by Han Feng; **141** photographer Tom Leighton/Roger Oates & Fay Morgan's house in Eastnor; **142** *a* Sabina Fay Braxton's apartment in Paris; **142** *bl, br* & **143** photographer James Merrell; **144** *l* Sheila Scholes' house near Cambridge; **144** *r* A house in South London designed by Todhunter Earle Interiors; **145** photographer Simon Upton/Mr & Mrs François von Hurter; **146** *l* photographer Polly Wreford/Mary Foley's house in Connecticut; **146-147** A house in Connecticut designed by Lynn Morgan Design; **148** Blakes Lodging designed by Jeanie Blake www.picket.com/blakesBB/blakes.htm; **149** *a* photographer Pia Tryde; **149** *b* photographer Sandra Lane; **150** *l* photographer James Merrell; **150** *r* photographer James Merrell/A house designed by Mary Drysdale; **151** photographer James Merrell/ Hotel de la Mirande, Avignon; **152** photographer James Merrell/A house designed by Mary Drysdale; **159** photographer James Merrel/Hotel Villa Gallici Aix en Provence, France; **160** photographer Simon Upton; **161** photographer James Merrell; **162** photographer Henry Bourne; **164** Laura Bohn's apartment in New York designed by Laura Bohn Design Associates; **167** photographer James Merrell/Svindersvik, Nacka, Stockholm; **168** photographer James Merrell/A house designed by Mary Drysdale; **172, 173** & **174** photographer James Merrell; **177** photographer Henry Bourne; **178** photographer James Merrell; **180** Sheila Scholes' house near Cambridge; **182** Sasha Waddell's house in London; **184** Designer of Modénature Henry Becq's apartment in Paris; **192** Annabel Astor's house in London is full of furniture and accessories designed exclusively for her OKA Direct Mail order catalogue.

Index